CONTENTS

Runaway American Dream

Listening to Bruce Springsteen

Da Capo Press
A Member of the Perseus Books Group

For my family

Designed by BookComp, Inc.
Set in 12.5 point Sabon

First Da Capo Press edition 2005
ISBN 0-306-81397-1

Published by Da Capo Press
A Member of the Perseus Books Group
www.dacapopress.com

Da Capo Press books are available at special discounts for bulk purchases in the U.S. by corporations, institutions, and other organizations. For more information, please contact the Special Markets Department at the Perseus Books Group, 11 Cambridge Center, Cambridge, MA 02142, or call (800) 255-1514 or (617) 252-5298, or e-mail special.markets@perseusbooks.com.

Library of Congress Cataloging-in-Publication Data

Guterman, Jimmy.
    Runaway American dream : listening to Bruce Springsteen / Jimmy Guterman.— 1st ed.
        p.   cm.
    ISBN 0-306-81397-1 (hardcover)
    ISBN 13: 978-0-306-81397-9
    1. Springsteen, Bruce.   2. Rock musicians—United States—Biography.
I. Title.
    ML420.S77G88 2005
    782.42166'092—dc22

                                                            2005008180

1 2 3 4 5 6 7 8 9—08 07 06 05

INTRODUCTION

Just what the world needs: another book about Bruce Springsteen.

There have been many dozens so far, ranging from picture books for children to picture books for adults, with biographies, critical studies, and reference books in between. The idea is to write a different kind of Bruce Springsteen book, one that focuses on the music, but not a book that only obsessive fans can appreciate. There have been a bunch of these, each attempting to tell the "real story," whatever that means. All have been unsatisfying, because they have been too insular to be generalized beyond a handful of Bruce Nuts. Most of them seem to have no agenda beyond "I think Bruce is great and maybe if I write a book about him I'll get to meet him or something."

The seven essays that follow focus on Springsteen's work and the times that created them. It doesn't scour the *National Enquirer* material—I really don't care why the guy's first marriage broke up—but the goal of the book is simple: to explore the many questions

Springsteen fans still have, 30 years down the road of his recording career. It's written from the point of view of a literate fan, but it's not another one of those "How Bruce's music changed my life" books. This is a book about Springsteen's work in which your Humble Author intends to play only a small role, but I can't pretend I'm not here writing it, that the art I'm considering isn't coming to you through the prism of my writing. Maybe my reaction to a work of art reflects interestingly on the art. Maybe it reflects interestingly on your response to the art. Maybe not. Whatever the interaction, please consider these lapses into first person a sign of enthusiasm rather than an order that anyone has to feel the same way about something as I do. I hate those works of criticism in which someone relies on "one would think" or "one would hear." The lapse into the vague third person is a way for a writer to do two stupid things simultaneously: distance himself or herself from the work in question and insist that the reader—the "one" in question—has to agree with everything the critic asserts. A good piece of critical writing is one side of a conversation, not a monologue. Please feel free to talk back, throw the book around the room, make fun of me, even agree now and then.

As I write this in March '05, it's certainly a time for disagreement among Springsteen fans. His October '04 tour headlining the Vote for Change caravan polarized his vast and diverse audience, just as the election polarized the planet. During his '84–'85 tour behind *Born in the U.S.A.*, Springsteen would often introduce a song (usually "Johnny 99," from the elemental *Nebraska*, but occasionally others) with a story about the value of friendship and community that ended with the moral "nobody wins unless everybody wins." At a time when he guessed he and the E Street Band were at their commercial peak, he was questioning how worthwhile his own commercial success really was. It changed the world for him and his bandmates, certainly. But it wasn't changing anything broader. The only thing surprising about Springsteen taking a very public stand in the '04 election was that it took so long.

Thanks to Bush's defeat of Kerry, for the first time in his career Springsteen found himself branded a loser. Of course, it's hard to be a loser if, as Springsteen claimed in his speech inducting U2 into the Rock and Roll Hall of Fame earlier this month, "I live an insanely expensive lifestyle that my wife barely tolerates." But Springsteen sees himself as an outsider, even when delivering a celebrity introduction to his fellow platinum-plated colleagues. Right after he boasted of his wealth, he said to the Waldorf-Astoria crowd, "I have a ludicrous image of myself that keeps me from truly cashing in." No one in rock'n'roll could be more mainstream than Springsteen. But even in front of a group of his peers, he sees himself standing outside.

That continues to play out in his work, too. The brand-new *Devils & Dust*, packed with older songs but much of it recorded in late '04 when it felt like the nation could go either way, is filled with the outsider voices that Springsteen's songs have employed as narrators since the very first song on his very first album. The new album is musically more diverse than *The Ghost of Tim Joad*. It's as if Springsteen experimented with how much he could flesh out solo-acoustic arrangements yet still have something that felt more like a solo album than an E Street affair. Steve Jordan's forceful, spare drums, for example, are the big reason the title number delivers more musically than just a regurgitation of the "Blood Brothers" melody. *Nebraska* notwithstanding, the guy makes better records when there are other musicians playing alongside him. Some of these outsider characters Springsteen lets speak for themselves, as in the uncensored nastiness of "Reno." Others speak with the benefit of Springsteen's intelligence. Characters like the soldier in the title track and the boxer in "The Hitter" relate their stories with a perspective far beyond what the real folks standing in their shoes would be likely to offer. *Devils & Dust* is full of songs that may not be literally true, but emotionally most of the tales are inarguable. And sometimes, as in "Long Time Comin'," he allows the narrator something approaching peace.

That peace may be fleeting, it may even be illusory, but Springsteen's work has long maintained that any respite from this dark world is a welcome one. Earlier this month the *Asbury Park Press* ran a short piece about several fans waiting outside the town's Convention Center while Springsteen rehearsed inside, preparing for the tour to support *Devils & Dust*. The fans waited more than three hours, listening to the muffled sounds within, before Springsteen emerged and signed some autographs for them on the way to his Range Rover. When Springsteen learned how long they had been waiting, he smiled and said, "You kids need to get a life." Get a life? What is it makes life worth living? Springsteen has been thinking about that on record and onstage for a long time now. This book hopes to follow Springsteen as he considers this question from many angles.

Jimmy Guterman
March 29, '05

Chapter 1

In the Shadow of The Boss

John Mellencamp is furious, and he's got a microphone in front of him. It's May '03, he says his record company isn't overjoyed by his recent political activism, and his days as a Top Ten hitmaker appear to be over. "What I haven't done, I don't think I can do. I don't think that there is time in my life left. And I don't—I think there's too much resistance to who I am to achieve what I thought I would be able to. The interesting thing about—there's a song on the new record about—song called 'Baltimore Oriole' that was written, in my mind, here in Bloomington, Indiana, by a guy from Bloomington, Indiana, a guy named Hoagy Carmichael. I didn't know this about Hoagy Carmichael, but he considered himself the poor man's Johnny Mercer. Never could get over the fact that Johnny Mercer got all the accolades, even though, you know, that's not really true.

At the end of the day, you know, his songs stack up to Mercer's easily. But Johnny Mercer was the guy. And Hoagy was, you know, kind of second string. I've always had that on my back. And so when I found out about Hoagy Carmichael, I was just like, 'Well, yeah.' You know, I look—I know other artists who feel that way. And a lot of us live here."

"Who's your Johnny Mercer?" Ken Paulson asks. Paulson's no dummy. A respected lawyer and journalist, he runs the First Amendment Center out of Vanderbilt. Soon he'll be named the top editor of *USA Today*. Clear-headed and experienced, he'll try to turn around McNewspaper in the wake of (a) the Jack Kelley fabrication scandal and (b) the fact that no one reads newspapers anymore. He's too much of a gentleman to let on that he knows who Mellencamp is talking about. Here, Paulson keeps his question short and direct, letting Mellencamp drive the conversation.

"Come on. It's so obvious. I'm not going to answer that if you can't answer it yourself. I'm like Hoagy Carmichael. I'll never be able to achieve what—I'll never be able to—how would somebody who was eloquent say that? I will never be able to see my star rise the way that I always thought it should have. Not gonna happen. So I have to accept it."

But Mellencamp doesn't sound like he's in a particularly accepting mood. Neither does Tom Petty. Like the former Johnny Cougar, Petty is a platinum rocker, responsible for some taut, angry, heartfelt, smart, mostly mainstream records, leading a sharp, focused, sometimes deliciously malevolent band through rock-radio playlists and large halls coast to coast. Along with Mellencamp, he's one of the few people to give "arena rock" a reasonably good name. It's September '79 and Petty is backstage at Madison Square Garden, where he's appearing as part of the "No Nukes" extravaganza. Petty is one of many worthy performers on the card: Jackson Browne, Ry Cooder, Bonnie Raitt, and Jesse Colin Young are here, too. There are a ton of meatheads here as well: The fey, vague, self-righteous would-be antinuclear anthems from John Hall and Graham Nash are enough to make you wish for a China syndrome that would make the music stop.

It's not the subpar performers who are bothering Petty. He and his band, the Heartbreakers, have performed a strong set—their cover of Solomon Burke's "Cry to Me," a song they've played since they were Florida locals known as Mudcrutch, would wind up a high point on a three-LP set documenting the "No Nukes" shows—but Petty sensed there was something wrong with the crowd at the Garden. They weren't entirely with him. In fact, it seemed like they were booing him.

They weren't booing him, he learns. They were *Brooocing* him. "What's the difference?" Petty asks, and walks off, in no need of an answer.

Mellencamp and Petty are testy, but Michael Stipe thinks it's pretty funny. "Peter?" he asks his guitarist through the microphone at the Gund Arena in Cleveland, "are we being . . . Brooced?" The singer for R.E.M., a band with hundreds of arena headline dates under its belt, realizes there's nothing he can do but smile. He's not going to change anything. He knows he fronts a fine band. He knows he can engage an arena crowd. But—unlike Mellencamp, who won't even speak Springsteen's name as if he was Lord Voldemort, or Petty, whose vanity is mixing with petulance—Stipe also knows that when you're on the same stage that Bruce Springsteen is going to be on, it's his stage, and there's nothing you can do but accept it. He laughs, starts into the next song, speaks to the crowd on his own terms. He'll never be Bruce Springsteen. But if he works at it, he can be a damn good Michael Stipe.

Alas, this evening, October 2, '04, feels like a night of genuinely diminished expectations. R.E.M. is sharing the bill with Bruce Springsteen and the E Street Band on the second night of American rock'n'roll's October surprise, the Vote for Change tour. Managed by one left-leaning PAC (MoveOn) and intended to fund another (America Coming Together), six sets of performers are crisscrossing the most high-profile swing states—among them, Pennsylvania, Ohio, Michigan, Minnesota, and Florida—bringing a message that is lukewarm-to-hot pro-Kerry and hot-to-scalding anti-Bush. The unsubtlety of the latter half of the message pops up in the brief set from tonight's first band, Bright Eyes, embodied by the young (he's 24 and

4

he's been recording for half his life), earnest, hyperverbal Conor Oberst, who declaims, "A vote for Bush is like shitting in your own bed." A charming simile, to be sure, but one only likely to appeal to the already converted. The bands that follow will have to do better. Either way, we're reduced to hoping rock stars will turn out the vote.

In the context of the cynical fall of '04, it's impossible to overstate the idealism fueling the Vote for Change tour and how out of step it is not only with the country at large, but with rock'n'roll at large. On the same day the Vote for Change caravan is in Cleveland to promote progressive voting, *Fortune* magazine is sponsoring its fourth annual Battle of the Corporate Bands a mile or so down the road at the Rock and Roll Hall of Fame and Museum. No, wiseass, it's not REO Speedwagon going up against Toto across from the enormous gift shop of the lifeless rock hall. (You know you're in trouble when the most engaging part of a rock'n'roll museum is a close look at a giant hot dog the members of Phish rode in.) The Battle of the Corporate Bands is an assemblage of eight bands representing companies ranging from eBay to Wells Fargo. The Nextel band, Direct Connectors, flew in on the corporate jet, if you were wondering. These adequate cover bands are not without their charms, but it's hard to feel any authentic rock'n'roll energy under signs that indicate the day's performances are taking place "with the rockin' support" of such countercultural icons as

5

KeyBank (Cleveland's hometown bank, with $89 billion in assets) and those crazy knuckleheads at that well-known Marxist stronghold Dodge.

If you want to take a break from exhibits that give equal weight to Bob Dylan and Bon Jovi, you can learn from the Battle of the Corporate Bands program that there's a "band showcase" through the morning and afternoon, followed by the actual invitation-only competition being held simultaneously with the Vote for Change event. At the same moment someone can register to vote at the Gund Arena, someone else can fill out a credit card application at the entrance to the Rock and Roll Hall of Fame and Museum. Which feels more like rock'n'roll to you?

It's not as easy a question as you might hope/think. This is a time when rock'n'rollers brag to members of other bands backstage about what a great deal they got with a corporate sponsor, when the idealists in U2 are portraying a rock'n'roll band in television ads for a computer company. The Rolling Stones aren't on the cover of *Rolling Stone* anymore; they're on the cover of *Fortune*.

The Gund Arena is nearly full, but listen around you and your ears will ring with evidence that many/most of your fellow attendees plopped down their $75 for the music, not the message. "I don't give a shit about all that," one of the fellows in the row behind me says. "I just wanna hear 'Rosalita.'" Springsteen is a performer who inspires loyalty in many of his fans, and this was

6

only the second time at a Springsteen show that I've heard a nonprofessional distance his affection for Springsteen's art from his distaste for the fundamental beliefs that ground the art. (The other time was in the cheap seats at Madison Square Garden in June '00, listening to two cops in the next row twist the song "American Skin [41 Shots]," an evenhanded dissection of race inspired by the fate of Amadou Diallo, into something with the subtlety of Ice-T's "Cop Killer.") Between sets, I heard a brother and a sister, both in their late 20s or early 30s, arguing over abortion. She had expressed reservations about Kerry but said she would vote for him because he took a pro-choice stand. "Abortion?" her brother asked incredulously and loudly. "Abortion? Since when did you even care about abortion?" It was, it seemed, an entirely new topic for them. What would come of this, I wondered.

People in the audience talking about politics at a rock'n'roll show: That's something you don't hear every night. But it's unlikely that politics will go far in a sports arena without actual entertainment. Remember Graham Nash at "No Nukes" with his hysterical tales of mutant sponges? All that made people change their minds on was whether it was time, at last, to get rid of their Graham Nash records.

And what of the entertainment tonight? Bright Eyes is on and off quickly, with Oberst squeezing what feels like 90 minutes' worth of words into a half-hour set. R.E.M., once a spunky quartet that lost its way along with its interest in writing fast songs when its drummer Bill Berry retired (name three songs from their latest record—see?), is performing a spirited set of obvious hits ("The One I Love," "Losing My Religion"), excerpts from its boring new record, and a lovely take of the geographically appropriate "Cuyahoga." But despite his extended lethargy in the studio, singer Michael Stipe has turned his onstage self into a sleeker version of Tom Waits in that many of the best parts of R.E.M.'s set tonight come between the songs when Stipe talks. Stipe started out onstage in the early eighties hiding behind his hair and lyrics that were either mumbles or nonsense syllables; now, resplendent in a white suit (with a Kerry t-shirt beneath to be revealed later) and shaved bald, he is as friendly a frontman as you could imagine, as cerebral as David Byrne but far looser, a mixture of humor and gravity, earnestness and silliness. He speaks drolly between songs, crumbling each page of notes and throwing it into the crowd after he reads it, name-checking Dennis Kucinich (Kerry doesn't get mentioned until late in the headliner's set), responding with humor to the inevitable Broocing.

At least at the end of R.E.M.'s set there arrives an acceptable reason for all the Broocing: Springsteen and his guitar are onstage with the band, closing the set with runs through "Bad Day" and "Man on the Moon." The latter is a surprising choice. It's a soft-focus tribute to Andy Kaufman, full of references to the late comic's obsession with professional wrestling and imitation of Elvis Presley, but this guided tour through one entertainer's weird professional obsessions is embedded in a truly openhearted and wistful arrangement and performance. Sure, professional wrestling and Elvis impersonations are junk we're celebrating, the music says, but it's our junk and why not celebrate it? (It's a more opaque version of the B-52s' similar, deeper "Deadbeat Club.") Springsteen isn't known to have mentioned Andy Kaufman onstage before, and his sober affinity with Elvis Presley dwelled mostly on The King as hit-or-miss role model and symbol of American dreams found, lost, and flushed down the toilet. Springsteen has performed many songs associated with Elvis and written a handful, but except for the never-released, rarely performed ditty "I'm Turning Into Elvis," he's never done so with humor. (OK, obsessives: Maybe he gets some points for invoking the "blessed name of Elvis" before he shoots out the television in "57 Channels [And Nothin' On]." But that's not a song about Elvis.) And here he is, Mr. Elvis-as-American-History-Lesson, standing beside Stipe as the Man in White does spastic Elvis impersonations.

Beneath the surface-level playing with Elvis's image, "Man in the Moon" is a song about wistful memory, and anyone who's heard "Bobbie Jean" realizes Springsteen knows what to do with that. Springsteen is in a supporting role during this song, even if he sings a verse and helps out the chorus. For most of the song he stands in front of the drum riser next to a dour-looking

Peter Buck, in friendly bar-band mode, modestly letting the band onstage call the shots, strumming along. But then, as often happens when a strong band reaches toward the conclusion of the set, the crowd singing along, the drummer kicking in harder, the excitement of the audience returning to the stage, "Man in the Moon" begins to soar. Stipe is so energized he perches precariously on a stage monitor and forgets the words to the song's last verse, cracking up half the band, and when he regains his physical and lyrical footing, he returns to the song with new verve. The song's sweetly melancholy coda, short on the record, comes in harder and the performers stay with it, Stipe howling and flailing his arms, bassist Mike Mills hopping with the enthusiasm of a child after ingesting a pillowcase full of Halloween candy, Springsteen pulling out brief, sliding solos that say more about the bittersweet memory of Kaufman and Presley than mere words.

And that's just the opening act. Between sets, as a pair of video screens play public service announcements featuring performers from the various Vote for Change packages, there's time to reflect on why, for musical reasons at least, it was a smart decision to go to the second night of the tour, rather than the previous night's kick-off in Philadelphia. Experience says the first night of a Springsteen tour is merely a template for what's to come. There tend to be amusing gaffes on opening night (Ann Arbor, '80: Springsteen starts with "Born to Run," forgets words; St. Paul, '84: opens second set by playing the same song twice to film a dud video), but people don't go to rock concerts, particularly those with $75-per-seat price tags, for amusing gaffes.

Shortly after 10:00 p.m., the house lights click off. No matter how many concerts you've been to, no matter how jaded you've become, there's still something exciting about that quick change that surprises and raises anticipation, even if you know the band plays the same songs in the same order every night. Maybe it's just a physical reaction. But tonight, when you're witnessing a performance by a band known in part for not playing the same songs in the same order every night, it's likely more than your nervous system adjusting to the dark.

After Stipe introduces them, the entire E Street Band comes onstage. There's the new kid, Soozie Tyrell, on violin. The two other members of the band with the least seniority, guitarist Nils Lofgren and singer Patti Scialfa, have been there for more than 20 years, which gives you a sense of how permanent membership is (even if those 20 years include a lengthy hiatus). Everyone else arriving onstage has played with Springsteen for 30 years or more. Lofgren's predecessor in the guitar slot, Steve Van Zandt, returned to the group in the late nineties, adding muscle and reclaiming his spot as Springsteen's onstage foil. Roy Bittan and Danny Federici and Garry Tallent and Max Weinberg make up the two pairs at the core of the E Street Band's sound: Bittan and Federici mix and match keyboard lines on opposite sides of the stage until they sound like one man with four hands, bassist Tallent and drummer Weinberg comprise a similarly empathic rhythm section. And then there's Clarence Clemons, the outsize saxophonist, the only member of the E Street Band to appear (at least part of him) on the front cover of a Springsteen record (twice!), the man whose few solos every night continue to be greeted by Pavlovian roars that sound like thunder.

They're quite a band, but right now they're just standing there. When he first decided he wanted to get involved publicly with the '04 election, a connection to electoral politics he hadn't attempted before, Springsteen intended to embark on a brief theater tour, just him and his guitar in a handful of swing states. But as his manager Jon Landau and his counterparts working for R.E.M., Pearl Jam, The Dave Matthews Band, and others explored what might make the most impact in the handful of states that might decide the presidential election, big noises from big arenas seemed more appropriate than small noises from small halls. So the stage is full, full of men and women holding their instruments and listening while Springsteen bends over his acoustic 12-string guitar and pulls out an idiosyncratic, Eastern-flavored "Star Spangled Banner." It's not so idiosyncratic that you can't hear the melody under the minor-key strums. He doesn't go for complete destruction of Francis Scott Key's war celebration that is the United States's national anthem in the spirit of Jimi Hendrix's electric Woodstock version. Rather, he is looking down at his black guitar, his face close to the top of the guitar neck, aching to extract something new and beautiful out of a song everyone on this planet knows too well. Yeah, we hold this song in common, the performance says, but we don't have to settle for it. It's a method not unlike that in the songs the optimistic-but-savvy Springsteen writes: searching for light in the darkness of insanity, in the words of a Nick Lowe song he and all the evening's performers will take on later. There's got to be something good in here, his performance says. All I have to do is look harder and play harder.

It's dark onstage except for the spotlight on Springsteen, but it's easy to see another guitar hanging around his neck behind him. It's an electric guitar, and it serves as a hint about the night: The performance will be tight, efficient, moving quickly from number to number. Indeed, the moment Springsteen finishes "The Star Spangled Banner," he signals the band to begin the drums-and-keyboard introduction to "Born in the U.S.A," kicking off a four-song full-band run with no pauses, each song moving inexorably into the next, carrying the set farther up the hill. They're not the lazy, clever segues you'd hear at a Grateful Dead show. Instead, they're the sounds of a man and a band trying to tell a coherent story about what the country is like, what is at stake this election season, and doing so with such ferocity that even those who don't care for Springsteen's politics can't help but be moved.

When Springsteen played "Born in the U.S.A." with the E Street Band on the '02–'03 tour supporting *The Rising*, he gave new life to the standard by extending it. It wasn't just the lyrical update ("30 years burning down the road" replaced the original 10-years post-Vietnam timecheck). Additions like Tallent's sliding bass lines and a fierce duel between Springsteen's guitar and Max Weinberg's drums that extended and extended, like a bungee cord getting pulled until the tension seemed to capture unlimited power, kept the song well off the oldies track. But tonight, the performance is all about terseness. Instead of its famous breakdown and recovery, "Born in the U.S.A." ends way early, at the moment of breakdown, smashing right into "Badlands."

If "Born in the U.S.A." is a concert standard, played often but not every night, "Badlands" is more of an obligatory part of a Springsteen set. That inevitability is not necessarily a good thing. Over the quarter century since the band first started playing it, "Badlands" has gainéd length but not depth. It has developed false endings and singalongs, but nothing to improve on its original construction. Indeed, Clemons's solo is still nearly note for note what it was when he first recorded it in '78. Pity for a moment the members of the E Street Band. They must feel like they've played this song every night since shortly after the ancestors of man crawled out of the primordial muck, and with each tour a great song gets a little bit flabbier, a little farther away from the tightly compressed original. This time out, with speed the rule, the song sounds different, airier. Springsteen's guitar solo squeezes in some more anger (unlike Clemons, he has found time over the intervening quarter century to toy with his brief break) and most of the fluff in the song has been excised: no false ending, no singalong, no coda after coda. Just direct expression. The same can be said of the two songs that follow, "No Surrender" and "Lonesome Day." The former has become a favorite of the Kerry campaign (the candidate arrives onstage to a recording of it); the latter, with some extra flourishes by Weinberg in the right unexpected places, ends the opening run.

The remainder of the main set has its ups and downs. There are calls to action between songs (no one will leave the arena without knowing that the deadline for voter registration is 4:00 p.m. on Monday). "The River" returns to its original arrangement (the band has gone at it many different ways over the years), ending with a striking falsetto; "Johnny 99," with Federici on accordion and Lofgren on lap steel, remains weird, a David Lynch hoedown, a jaunty tale of a man begging a judge who has sentenced him to life to execute him instead; a soul-scraping "Youngstown" in which Lofgren, eyes closed, seemingly in a trance, reinvents the jagged solo that was a highlight of the band's '99–'00 reunion tour, somehow making it sound even darker.

The mood shifts when "special guest" John Fogerty appears, carrying a baseball bat–shaped guitar. Some of the magnificent songs Fogerty wrote and performed in the late sixties with Creedence Clearwater Revival seem eerily and unhappily prescient about this dark moment: "Bad Moon Rising" and "Fortunate Son" in particular, but Fogerty's sly, suggestive songwriting style made even songs that weren't about What Lousy Shape The World Is In lend themselves to that interpretation.

Before he opens his mouth, it's hard not to think about Fogerty's long-ago masterpieces and how contrary his brilliant method was to the ruling culture—and the ruling counterculture. At a time when stretching out was all the rage, Fogerty opted for a defiant concision that made his band's music timeless when much of the trendier material from the late sixties now sounds silly. Wordiness and extended jams were rarely a part of Creedence Clearwater Revival's mix: Fogerty grew up on lanky rockabilly records from Memphis and loping rhythm-and-blues 45s from New Orleans—he admired the firmness in those cuts and sought to say what needed to be said plainly and then move on. He didn't have time for bullshit, and he assumed that his audience didn't either. Although tautness was a virtue in Fogerty's heart and mind, he wasn't afraid to speak metaphorically. (When he finally succumbed to the long jam, on a trip through Marvin Gaye's "I Heard It Through the Grapevine," he found a way to sound terse and speedy for a longer time.) In songs like "Who'll Stop the Rain," "Proud Mary," and "Run Through the Jungle," among many other hits, he opted for a grand generality. As long as he worked in the constraints of potential hit singles, Fogerty could thrive (as soon as the other members of Creedence Clearwater Revival were allowed to write their aimless songs, the group shattered). "I wrote a song for everyone," Fogerty sang. That was his most wide-eyed dream, and the one he could achieve only by speaking from heart to heart. His rough voice was nobody's idea of pretty, but his gruff, resilient tenor worked because of its total confidence and lack of pretension. (His tenor has gotten higher and higher over the years, apparently not intentionally.)

"Centerfield," the song Fogerty plays with his Louisville Slugger six-string, isn't one of those top-ranked Creedence songs. It's from the '85 album of the same name, the first of his three when-I-get-around-to-it comebacks, and the only one that was commercially successful. Even the most memorable of Fogerty's eighties and nineties songs (like "The Old Man Down the Road," "Change in the Weather," and "Premonition") refer to Creedence Clearwater tunes, and their power is borrowed from memories of the earlier songs, not earned themselves. "Centerfield," one of Fogerty's few top-drawer light songs, is a welcome, energetic mood-changer midway through the set, but it's not like the unparalleled chronicler of Vietnam and Nixon has been grafted onto the bill for the Vote for Change tour because he writes good songs about baseball.

He was brought out, to some degree, to play his new antiwar song, "Déjà Vu (All Over Again)," but that turns out to be the night's low point. It's a poor retread of the *Centerfield*-era "I Saw It On T.V.," which was itself a poor retread of the Creedence classic "Who'll Stop the Rain." It's an image that loses clarity each time it goes through the photocopier. Ten songs into Springsteen's set, it's the first time everyone in the Gund Arena crowd has sat down (that's right; thousands stood through the ballad "The River"). The band valiantly tries to kick it up, but the song's third-hand observations and clichés (the first verse alone, a mere four lines, features writing on the wall, a voice inside you, and "you've heard it all before") go nowhere slowly. It's not just the audience sitting down. Clemons sits on a chair at his end of the stage and he can barely work up enough enthusiasm to tap his unmiked tambourine.

Fogerty's place on the bill is justified by a hot, harsh "Fortunate Son." When he performed the song during his Creedence peak, Fogerty sang and played the song hard but stood in front of the microphone as if his work boots were nailed to the stage floor. Tonight, he's stalking the stage from end to end, exhorting the audience to sing along and the band to play harder, finally in control and all over the place at once. "Fortunate Son" is an unruinable composition—even Bob Seger couldn't smother it when he dropped a holiday-dinner portion of meat-and-potatoes on the song—and it's one of those Fogerty songs that's both timeless and as of the moment as tomorrow's newspaper. "Fortunate Son," a tumultuous rocker, may be one of the angriest songs written about the United States and one of the most patriotic. A cry for truth, a shout for fairness, a scream against unearned privilege, "Fortunate Son" was composed around the time George W. Bush skipped National Guard assignments, and it's a far more precise critique of W's current presidency than the "Déjà Vu" song most of the crowd has forgotten already. The E Street Band doesn't share Creedence's unsubtle wallop, but a month before the election there's no time for subtlety and its members—particularly an excited Weinberg—play as if a snare drum hit just right harder than ever before might just swing a vote. Fogerty isn't in anyone's shadow; he's leading the band through his song.

Such moments tend to evaporate pretty quickly, and this is no exception. Next up is a Fogerty-Springsteen duet on "The Promised Land" that feels like the antithesis to the earlier "Badlands." It's another song of the same vintage ('78's *Darkness on the Edge of Town*), but this time the extra 25 years of bloat is there for all to hear. Fogerty's purified tenor is a good fit for the song, but the song feels old tonight. For a night that's supposed to be about looking forward, that's not a good idea.

After a tear through "The Rising," complete with the same vocal choreography from the last tour, made somehow more dramatic by the image of Tallent hugging his bass during the breakdown, and a spirited "Because the Night" in which Michael Stipe returns, sings his friend Patti Smith's lyrics as opposed to Bruce's original, and drops to his knees in not-at-all-mock homage during Springsteen's guitar solo, Bruce calls for "Mary's Place" and takes a break while the band performs the song's airy intro.

Now let's wait a minute. "Mary's Place," from '02's *The Rising*, is not the worst song Springsteen has written and recorded. I'll let the true crazies nominate candidates for that appellation, but I suppose if we do open the voting we'll hear about "Mary, Queen of Arkansas," "The Angel," and half of the '92 crime against his fans, *Human Touch*. "Mary's Place" isn't that bad, but it is certainly the worst song Springsteen directs the E Street Band to play every night, the worst song he felt was worth putting on his *Essential* compilation, and the worst song that wastes 15 to 20 precious minutes of a set every night he plays it. In this book's final section I'll venture a guess as to why Springsteen might love this bad song so much, but for now what's important is that Springsteen is using "Mary's Place," the unlikely 9/11 party song, to carry way more than its feeble bones can support. It includes a rare unfunny rap (sample line: "The E Street Band can take you to the river of change and take you to the other side"). He's often hilarious when he affects a preacher's delivery, but not tonight. His claims that the Democratic platform includes promises of on-time pizza delivery, free beer in every home, and a ban on cellphone communications fall flat. And the set piece during the breakdown, when Springsteen pulls a bow-tied man from the pit in front of the stage, offers to turn the alleged swing voter to the Democratic side, and "heals" the plant by having the crowd chant "Halley-burton" three times, is as unfunny to much of the crowd as the promise of Four More Years. Should Springsteen ever tour again with the E Street Band, he's likely to rethink the structure of his set. Sometimes longtime standards have to be reconfigured: He performed "Born to Run" solo acoustic on the tour supporting *Tunnel of Love*. Sometimes, as when "Rosalita" disappeared from his set list for more than a decade, they have to be retired for a time. It's time to pull the trigger on "Mary's Place."

Without the light rhythms of "Mary's Place" to hold him down, Springsteen can move more comfortably into campaign-rally mode. "Now everybody's favorite part of the show," he says after the song fades away. "The public service announcement!" He laughs, but quickly turns serious, looking down at the words on a monitor buried in the stage floor to make sure he gets it right.

"We remain a land of great promise. But it's time we need to move America towards the fulfillment of its promises that she's made to her citizens: economic justice, civil rights, protection of the environment, respect for others, and humility in exercising our power at home and around the world. These core issues of American identity are what's at stake on November 2. I believe that Senator Kerry and Senator Edwards understand the important issues and I think they're prepared to help our country move forward. America is not always right. That's a fairy tale that you tell your children at night before they go to sleep. But America is always true. And it's in seeking those truths that we find a deeper patriotism. Don't settle for anything less. We've got some work to do between now and Election Day. If you share our concerns, find the best way to express yourself, roll up your sleeves, and get out there and do something. And remember, the country we carry in our hearts is waiting."

With that last line, echoing the tag of his recent op-ed piece in the *New York Times*, Springsteen counts to four and the band smashes into a big, loud "Born to Run," made a bit bigger and louder by the arrival onstage of R.E.M.'s Peter Buck and Michael Mills. Buck stands back near the drum and piano risers. He has changed clothes since his band's set and he appears to be wearing either striped pajamas or a tailored hotel awning. He remains sober-faced, while Mills, his long curls flying as he jumps, appears to have raided everyone else's Halloween take since last we saw him. He's both performer and fan, embodying the energy and purpose the Vote for Change performers hope to engender in the arena, most of whom appear to have been of voting age at least since the Carter administration. That mood carries into the encore, which starts with a sharp rollick through the Creedence classic "Bad Moon Rising" and climaxes (or you think it is at the time) with an all-cast (there are 17 people on stage) version of

"(What's So Funny 'Bout) Peace, Love, and Under-standing," Nick Lowe's ironic examination of hippie values that lost all its irony when Elvis Costello and the Attractions recorded their definitive version of it in '78 on *Armed Forces*. (Go buy it right now if you don't have it.) Costello's version, aside from including the most forceful rhythm guitar solo in the history of rock-'n'roll, is at once both angry and idealistic, so it's no accident that it's Costello's version, not Lowe's, that serves as the template for tonight's version, with Spring-steen, Fogerty, and Oberst sharing the verse. There's nothing funny about peace, love, and understanding, but there's great fun and purpose in celebrating it. And, as the song rises through chorus after chorus, it's cele-bration that the performance captures most of all, from Weinberg's fluid rolls to Oberst's convulsive pogo dance. Springsteen, alternately smiling during the instrumental breaks and clenching his eyes shut as he sings, stays close to the ground amid the hopping and bounding about him. Someone, after all, has to.

You'd think that would be it, that would be what the bands wanted on fans' and voters' minds as they left the hall, but there's one more. When people talk about the E Street Band as majestic, they're talking about performances like tonight's opening up of Patti Smith's "People Have the Power." Those familiar with the song recognize it as the purposeful first salvo of her delightful '88 comeback album *Dream of Life*, a rock-ing meditation on what the vox populi can do that satisfied both the eggheads and spiritualists in her audience, a call that satisfied both the head and the heart. Her recorded version is spacious, winning rock'n'roll, as is what fills the hall as the clock strikes midnight, but for a moment all I hear in my memory is a version I heard her sing on television once, I don't even remember when, it must have been more than a decade ago, but it was just her and her (now late) husband Fred Smith, armed with just her voice and his guitar, at some otherwise-forgettable awards show. I was never a particularly devoted fan of either Smith, but I do remember how their acoustic performance moved me.

As I heard the rock'n'roll of "People Have the Power" tumble around me in Cleveland, I flashed back to the moments that did it for me back when it was just Mr. and Mrs. Smith performing to television cameras. There were two. About halfway through the song, she started a verse with "Where there were deserts, I saw fountains" and, then and now, it felt like in a mere seven words, Patti Smith was able to summarize what art is supposed to do, transform the everyday into something more, something only she could see, something she was now intent on sharing with all who would (could?) hear. It's not unlike what Springsteen has devoted his career to, at least since *Darkness on the Edge of Town*, when he discovered the lyrical and musical concerns that fuel his work to this day. He sees the enchanted in the everyday life and the everyday riff. Behind the desert of working-class defeat in a song like

"Badlands," he can sense something brighter, something worth fighting for. You can hear it in the music, not just the words. Smith is supposed to be some art figure and Springsteen a comparatively artless bard, but there's more than one hit song that ties them together. They're looking for the fountains and finding them.

And the other moment? At the end of the song, during a final extended chorus, Smith stops her lyrics and shouts, simply and directly, "LISTEN!" Stipe, an ardent and public Smith fan, gets to sing that order and the lines that follow it:

I believe everything we dream can come to pass
    through our union
We can turn the world around
We can turn the earth's revolution
We have the power
People have the power . . .

Separated from the music, those words can seem mere slogan, too easy, naïve. But these are rock lyrics, not lines of poetry, and whether put across by 17 rockers on a packed arena stage or two wan figures on an otherwise empty stage, the sound of a voice and a guitar (if not much more) pushing it along gives power and clarity. And, if you're in Cleveland, along with 20,000 others, many of whom are singing the chorus, it's hard not to get swept along by the conviction of the words and the singers. As Joey Ramone sang, it feels like something to believe in. Why not believe in rock'n'roll? What's the competition: politics? *Politics*? As Springsteen said famously onstage in Los Angeles in '85 before ripping into Edwin Starr's "War," "Blind faith in your leaders, or in anything, will get you killed." For all the pro-Kerry talk, it's hard to believe that the senator who's for the death penalty and against gay marriage, who voted for both the Iraq War and the Patriot Act, is the first choice of many of the people on the stage, all of whom have expressed traditional progressive stands. But he's the best choice right now, they reckon, as do millions of others (in what other election would there be a group called Kerry Haters for Kerry?). It's easy to be swept along, but it's also easy to recall John Kenneth Galbraith's truism about politics being a choice between the disastrous and the unpalatable. Or, as *The Economist* put it shortly after this show, a choice in this election between the incoherent and the incompetent. As the night ends with the house lights up, thousands of people chanting "People have the power," and a grinning Stipe holding his Kerry t-shirt taut so people will see it better, it's easier to believe in the music far more than any mere politician. These musicians have come together to advance a politician, but they leave the stage proving more than anything that the feeling you get when you leave a rock concert can be more inspiring than anything a politician can offer. As the night ends and you file out of the arena, who do you believe more? Who do you believe at all?

You don't need an arena stage to deliver a rock'n'roll show worth believing in. Performers as diverse as the Flatlanders, the Roches, and the Mekons, acts who headline arenas only in their dreams, play with an intensity and a conviction that are undeniable. On their best nights, they make an audience feel like they'd follow the bands anywhere. They're stuck in halls too small to contain their talent, but they plug in and plug on.

And what of the arena-worthy performers we visited not so many pages back? John Mellencamp is a rich rock star, has no trouble selling his awful paintings, and shares his life with a model. He'll even kick off the Washington, D.C., stop of the Vote for Change tour and share a microphone (briefly) with The Boss. Tom Petty gets to work with some of the greatest rock-'n'rollers ever. Michael Stipe sounds like he's had enough therapy not to be unnerved when he's Brooced. But imagine yourself at a bar late one night, in a stuffed club, seeing a band that's never going to even get a shot at a record deal. Then think about the guys onstage.

Many Springsteen fans have had the opportunity to think about those guys onstage, even if they were waiting for another guy. I remember seeing them, in the early eighties, '82 to be specific, during many, many late

Sunday nights that spilled over into many, many early Monday mornings. Quite a few had some tedious day job or summer-college job to return to in six or seven hours, but there we were, on a hunch. And the hunch had nothing to do with the musicians we had paid to hear.

The Stone Pony on Ocean Avenue is not the sort of place most of us would choose to be on a cool early autumn night. The dance floor is sticky, not that there's enough room for any of us to dance much. And this isn't a pogoing crowd: The people here, most of them men, are too old to be punks, more likely to dig Billy Joel than Johnny Rotten. The weather outside is doing what the Jersey shore tends to around midnight: The oppressive heat disappears in a flash, replaced by winds that come off the shore, past the boardwalk, and across Ocean Avenue, repeatedly extinguishing the cigarettes of people waiting in line to get into the club, which is already packed to the point that the Fire Marshall ought to take notice.

Chances are we don't much care for the band onstage right now, even if they are the headliners, the folks we paid $7 to see. Like most of the people so close around us, we are here on a hunch, not to witness some adequate cover band. "Mustang Sally" and "Lucille" are wonderful songs, and they're performed tonight loudly and with spirit, although what's onstage doesn't come within shouting distance of the Wilson Pickett and Little Richard originals. We yawn, look at our watches, wonder whether this is worth it.

28

Unless, that is, one particular friend of the band shows up, as he has seven of the past 13 Sunday nights. Some time—right around now, we've all noted either to each other or ourselves—Bruce Springsteen has parked his dark blue Camaro a block or so away from the Stone Pony, walked in, grabbed a beer, picked up a guitar, plugged in, and turned a passable bar band into the backing for some of the most unruly six-string bending and edge-of-the-throat shouting we've ever heard.

There he is. Everyone's looking at Springsteen—tan in a red muscle-t, eyes clenched shut and eyebrows dancing up and down as he solos again and again—but there are half a dozen guys onstage with him. The lights shine on them, too. They're sweating and working hard, too. But no one is looking at them. Tonight the band is Cats on a Smooth Surface, an agreeable enough cover band (they wrote some originals, but it was their spirited versions of familiar material that earned them a local following). They played the Stone Pony regularly, often on Sunday nights. Led by guitarist and singer Bobby Bandiera, they were adequate and enjoyable. On the nights when their celebrity buddy was not expected, you could listen, dance, enjoy, maybe even send up a barbed request. Their repertoire, after all, extended from the Isley Brothers to Billy Idol.

Ask the band members how they feel. "The crowd didn't care about us," one told me at the time. "Hated it," another chimed in. Then they both urged me not to write any of this down, because they didn't want to say anything negative that might get back to Springsteen. As Cats member Glen Burtnick did finally tell someone else for publication, "People would rush the stage, suddenly, they would just rush the stage because they wanted to have the best seat in the house for if and when Springsteen would get up on stage and jam with us. They would stand there for an hour or so, waiting and waiting and waiting. It was pretty strange. It was like playing a funeral or something, until Springsteen got up."

The year '82 was a time of transition for Springsteen, a time when he was immersed in the start-and-stop sessions (lasting to '84) that would yield *Born in the U.S.A.*, a time when he had to rethink everything from his band to his audience. As far as outsiders knew, he was just working, working, working, taking a break from one of his marathon studio campouts. His latest album, *Nebraska*, that unexpected set of acoustic tunes chronicling desperation both quiet and explosive, was considered an aberration, brilliant but self-indulgent. Here, onstage, screaming "Lucille" and "Twist and Shout," he was a big rock'n'roller again. He was bigger physically, too: in that sweaty t-shirt, the scrawny seventies rocker now looked more like the overbuilt Sylvester Stallone as John Rambo in last year's *First Blood*.

He'd have 100 percent of the crowd's attention even if he still looked like he belonged on the "before" side of the Charles Atlas ad. This is a guy with a Number

One album ('80's *The River*, his most recent full-band outing) and a truckload of arena sellouts under his belt. He could be playing anywhere tonight, but he's here. Not for long, though. After barely 40 minutes onstage, Springsteen would put down his guitar, slap the hands of the members of Cats on a Smooth Surface and those in the front of the crowd, walk back to his Camaro, and return home. Soon, the members of Cats would be standing on the stage in an emptied club, breaking down their instruments while the club's staff cleaned the dance floor.

Springsteen got quite a bit from these outings—it kept him loose, connected to playing rock'n'roll while the dispersed members of the E Street Band were unavailable. It's unclear what Cats got out of it tonight. Their take from the door or the bar was higher than usual, I suppose, but it's not like they were going to be able to parlay the notoriety of being Springsteen's some-time bar-stage accompanists into much more than what they enjoyed right now. (Several of the members of the band would go on to varying levels of success individually, but Cats would remain Shore-band footnotes.)

Some units did benefit from being in the shadow of The Boss. Around the same time Cats worked on its Sunday-night residency, the Rhode Island sextet Beaver Brown, which had picked up something of a Shore following thanks to its sub–E Street approach (best captured in their '80 independent single "Wild Summer Nights" b/w "Tender Years"), got lucky. Led by guitarist and songwriter John Cafferty, even the band's song titles sounded like parodies of Springsteen songs: "On the Dark Side," "Down by the Cove," "Voice of America's Sons." Cafferty's gruff Springsteen-soundalike voice got his band a gig writing the music for the '83 film *Eddie and the Cruisers*, which despite a nuanced performance by Tom Berenger as a music-prodigy-turned-teacher was in fact a piece of crap about the dead singer of Berenger's long-ago band, the Cruisers, trying to communicate from beyond the grave (don't ask). The movie tanked but was a launching pad for a brief hitmaking career: one hit single, some good-paying soundtrack jobs, among them the inevitable *Eddie and the Cruisers II: Eddie Lives!*, which sounds like a horror movie (or an Iron Maiden album) and sort-of is. It's unclear whether the Springsteen-soundalike elements of Cafferty's voice, songs, arrangements, and performances were coincidental or intentional, but they were amusing. When asked to write a blues riff by the Eddie and the Cruisers producers, he came up with a variation on Springsteen's "Adam Raised a Cain" blues riff. It would have been funny if the music had been better. For that, listen to the versions of "Take Me Out to the Ball Game" and the theme to *The Flintstones* credited to "Bruce Springstone" for a delightful example of the satirist illuminating the satirized. Weird Al, listen up!

Beaver Brown was only the most grotesque example of what happened when living in the shadow of Springsteen could turn into living in the reflected glory of The

Boss. Cafferty and Co. enjoyed a bit of success, but some masterful performers had the bad luck to be compared, constantly, with one of the greats. In a better world, Joe Grushecky would live in a mansion down the road from Springsteen's. Instead, this enormous talent spends his days teaching some of western Pennsylvania's most troubled children. Twenty-five years after his first record, he's amazingly consistent on disc. He made great records early in his career, and he's making great records now. It doesn't get much better than the last two, *Fingerprints* and *True Companion*. Who do you know who has made back-to-back great albums more than 20 years ago, and is doing the same thing now? There's Dylan, Lucinda Williams, Neil Young, Springsteen, maybe a few more. He's on that level.

But almost no one knows. You'd think they would have had they heard his '80 breakthrough with his band, the Iron City Houserockers, *Have a Good Time (But Get Out Alive)*. When punk crested on these shores in the late seventies, it was hard for a decidedly old-wave bar band to be heard as anything other than a throwback. Journeymen like the Iron City Houserockers had to get smarter. If their concern for workaday disillusions and fleeting escape through the pickup-truck radio wasn't exactly anarchy in motion, they had to show potential trendsetting fans nationwide that it wasn't just low-budget arena pomp, either. And the Iron City Houserockers pulled it off. *Have a Good Time (But Get Out Alive),* the second of the Pittsburgh sextet's four albums in their original incarnation, is fierce and admonishing. In songs like "Don't Let Them Push You Around," "Pumping Iron," and "We're Not Dead Yet," Grushecky's raging chronicles of commonplace urban loss tumble amidst an avalanche of guitars. No surprise there: The album was produced by guitar-rock kings Ian Hunter and Mick Ronson, with an assist from a certain Steve Van Zandt. In "Blondie," longtime fan Grushecky tells of saving up for scalped tickets and feels betrayed that "Now they're playing your song in all those places/That won't let me and Angela in." This was the first, and still about the only, American rock-'n'roll song to explicitly question the merchandising of "new wave" to the paying customers. Cutting deeper are the pairing of "Old Man Bar" and "Junior's Bar." In the slow, deliberate "Old Man Bar," pianist Gil Snyder growls out the tale of a young steelworker listening to World War II veterans repeating battle tales; in the "Junior's Bar" treatment, over the same melody, Grushecky is at another tavern, desperate to connect, terrified to make a move. All these characters—steelworkers, retirees, bank robbers, dole walkers, drunks—end up crushed, muttering warnings for those about to face the wheel. This bloodied defiance linked the Iron City Houserockers to punk; it also suggested that the mainstream didn't have to be the home of the spayed anymore.

The album was beginning-to-end spectacular, yet it never even entered the *Billboard* Top Two Hundred

Albums Chart. Grushecky shared many of Springsteen's concerns and built his sound from similar, albeit bluesier, sources, and was certainly more worthy of a hit than Beaver Brown. Alas, Grushecky had too much originality to be considered in the shadow of you-know-who. Springsteen sensed in Grushecky a kindred spirit (the same summer he was jumping onstage with Cats on a Smooth Surface, he was joining the Houserockers in a Red Bank club for an encore of Chuck Berry's "Bye Bye Johnny"), and in the mid-nineties wrote more than an album's worth of songs with Grushecky, some of which ended up on Grushecky's '95 album *American Babylon*, which Springsteen produced. Some of their other collaborations have ended up in sundry places. "Code of Silence," a tough-minded relationship song, wound up on a Springsteen rarities disc and earned a Grammy; "The Wall," about Maya Lin's Vietnam memorial in Washington, D.C., has been played live a couple of times; and there are many more.

Most amusing of the collaborations may be "Idiot's Delight," which surfaced on Grushecky's '98 *Coming Home*. It's got a good beat, you can dance to it, and it can be read as an indictment of the poor sons of bitches who crowd Jersey shore clubs late at night. Only a fan in denial wouldn't allow that interpretation. It's overtly a song about St. Peter looking down from wherever he is at us wretched humans, but it's not hard to make the interpretive leap. And one night in particular, the writers almost certainly meant it that way, at least in part.

The weekend after the '04 election, when most Americans who went to the polls apparently decided not to Vote for Change, Grushecky and Springsteen played a charity show at—where else?—the Stone Pony, and they played "Idiot's Delight" together. After the show's organizer, Grushecky manager Bob Benjamin, thanked Springsteen for his Vote for Change work, some in the crowd switched on a chant of "Four more years!" Those onstage either didn't hear it or pretended not to hear it, but this was far from the only night that someone on the stage at the Stone Pony might have felt some anger toward the paying audience—even if it was for a new reason.

Grushecky may have been the most gifted of those in the shadows, but the performer with the deepest roots in Shore clubs, the one who lived a parallel but subordinate career for many years, was Southside Johnny Lyon, a tremendous soul and blues singer, a sterling harmonica player, and a man whose career flourished under the sponsorship of not only Springsteen but also Springsteen's Dean Martin, Steve Van Zandt.

Southside Johnny Lyon is the American equivalent of Graham Parker, and not just because of their occasional vocal similarities. Both approach their music as a life-or-death proposition, both got that idea from the amazing commitment to material they heard in sixties rhythm-and-blues records recorded in Memphis and Muscle Shoals, and both were energized by punk although neither were punks. At their cores, Lyon and

Parker were soul singers. Parker enjoyed a brief Bruce connection (trading compliments and dueting with The Boss on Parker's *Up Escalator* record), but Lyon was playing beside Springsteen back during the Nixon era.

Consider, briefly, the '78 album *Hearts of Stone* by Southside Johnny and the Asbury Jukes. After two good-to-very-good albums (*I Don't Want to Go Home* and *This Time It's for Real*) that presented soul classics alongside new sacrifices to the tradition by old pals Springsteen and Van Zandt, the Jukes recorded the greatest soul record to ever come out of New Jersey. Everything on *Hearts of Stone*, particularly the writing (no oldies here, just nine Van Zandt and Springsteen originals) and the production (by Van Zandt), was more taut and less constrained by what the band had already been able to achieve onstage. The Asbury Jukes had improved tremendously in terms of discipline and stamina, but they did get help from some ringers: E Street Band drummer Max Weinberg pushes the beat throughout. And who's the singer responding to Lyon's call on "Trapped Again"? Whoever played what (as with so many albums, you can ignore the list of credits on the back cover if you're looking for accuracy or completeness), the band swiftly burrows inside these songs, most of them romanticized tales of fractured love, and leads Lyon to their souls. Not that Lyon needs any help. His singing on *Hearts of Stone* is his least chatty and his most believable, and his artless gruffness makes his and Van Zandt's soul dreams come true.

Let us now praise Southside Johnny and the Asbury Jukes, defiant performers, true to their musical ideals at a time when real blues and soul have zero commercial chance. (Remember the late seventies? *Grease*? The Blues Brothers? Supertramp? Toto?) There can't be any reason to play this music but love. The occasional song got played on FM rock stations in a handful of likely markets like New York, Philadelphia, and Cleveland, but this was highly emotional music played for highly emotional reasons. As Springsteen wrote in his liner notes to Southside's debut, *I Don't Want To Go Home*, "I brought up a lot of the past in these notes, and I hope Johnny don't [sic] mind, but I think it's time to bring it up before it's lost forever, because I know pretty soon it'll all be gone." The Jukes were trying to keep a romanticized art form alive.

The Jukes were also a bit of an Art Project for Springsteen and Van Zandt. With the Jukes, Van Zandt could play the auteur role unavailable in his steady job as the second guitarist in the E Street Band. And Springsteen could enjoy an alternate career, deploying songs he decided weren't worth putting on his own records or reviving songs like "You Mean So Much to Me" and "When You Dance" from his earlier prerecording career, songs that would sound like juvenilia in an E Street context but worked beautifully with the Jukes.

How could Lyon not have been chafing? Lyon and Jukes guitarist Billy Rush were both songwriters, yet none of the 29 songs on the band's first three records had been anything but soul covers or interpretations of Springsteen and Van Zandt compositions (to be fair, Lyon did enjoy one actual co-writing credit, along with Bruce and Steve, on *Hearts of Stone*). Working under Van Zandt and Springsteen's tutelage got them a record deal and attention, but it was time for them to grow up and write their own songs. So they recorded two modestly successful records, *The Jukes* ('79) and *Love Is a Sacrifice* ('80). The cover art of the former featured Lyon standing in front of a green background that Owen O'Donnell calls the "Wall of Slime"; the latter highlighted two backup singers named Patti and Soozie who would play different but important roles in the Springsteen story over the next decades. The band remains a compelling live force (see it yourself some time; the live *Reach Up and Touch the Sky* from that era is too disjointed to capture the energy and the passion). Alas, the group has fallen apart on record. They go into the studio every few years, crank out OK versions of OK songs (many by former Cats guitarist Bobby Bandiera, who's been a Juke since the mid-eighties), none of which are heard by anyone but diehards. The only beginning-to-end strong record they've recorded since *Hearts of Stone* came out in '91 and it's called *Better Days*. The producer's name is Van Zandt, the bass player's name is Tallent, the drummer's name is Weinberg, and nine of its 11 songs were written by Van Zandt or Springsteen.

Springsteen started off his career in the shadow of Bob Dylan. He didn't do much to discourage people from thinking of him as the latest in a long line of New Dylans: "Blinded by the Light," the first song on his first album, opens with a torrent of Dylanesque images, lines that giddily go on way too long, that make the latest New Dylan, Conor Oberst (aka Bright Eyes), seem laconic in comparison. But Springsteen quickly transcended his sticky situation by differentiating himself from his frank role model. Most of the New Bruces haven't done that. When they get the chance to step out of the shadow, it often turns out that they can't (Beaver Brown) or they do so to at best mixed results (Southside Johnny). Sometimes the shadow is so thick that a large audience can't discover a significant, original talent (Joe Grushecky).

Why does this happen? It's not just the combination of popularity and longevity. If that were the case, we'd be confronted with performers who can't escape the shadow of, say, Aerosmith or Van Halen, two hard-rock bands of varying stripes who've been around selling lots of records for decades. Guns N' Roses quickly developed from Aerosmith clone to original band, for example (despicable, yes, but original). When you see Springsteen take the stage with another band, be it R.E.M. in an airy arena or Cats on a Smooth Surface in a smoky club, his personality and authority become the center. You could see it even when Springsteen was warming up crowds in the last days of the Kerry campaign. He is doomed to be the center. Established performers such as Jackson Browne and Bob Seger, who had careers as recording artists before Springsteen entered Columbia Records executive John Hammond's office, felt their music change dramatically after they heard Springsteen. Like his rock'n'roll forebears the Beatles, the Rolling Stones, and Bob Dylan, Springsteen changed the rules of rock'n'roll, immodestly tried to expand what rock'n'roll could do. And he changed it without changing much himself. He hasn't embarrassed himself musically (*Human Touch* is a bad record, but it's no *Self-Portrait*). He's stayed focused on what he's good at: no paintings for sale, no rock operas, no songs sold for TV advertisements. But the flip side to that lack of embarrassment is his musical conservatism. Indeed, perhaps the most devastating criticism one could work up about Springsteen is that he hasn't changed much in the more than 30 years since he started recording. Dylan's world includes both "Song to Woody" and "Love Sick." Each of Dylan's many reinventions yields new generations of imitators—and then Dylan leaves them behind. Springsteen is nowhere near as diverse.

He's also nowhere near as inconsistent. On the last night of the E Street Band's '02–'03 world tour, in front of a cold, wet Shea Stadium crowd, Springsteen kicked off the final encore by rolling out Bob Dylan. The band leaned into a shuffle that turned out to be "Highway 61 Revisited," one of Dylan's most lasting compositions. But it was an off night for Dylan, who at different times seemed to be playing a different key, a different tempo, or a different song from everyone else on the stadium stage. It was a six-minute long train wreck, during which Dylan sometimes sang and played with intensity and sometimes seemed about to fall down. Springsteen grinned throughout the song, nodding extra hard as if to support his idol. Springsteen rarely trades in the insanity that's at the core of even a coherent version of "Highway 61 Revisited," with gonzo couplets like "Well Georgia Sam he had a bloody nose/Welfare Department they wouldn't give him no clothes."

One week in October '89, I saw Bob Dylan perform at the Opera House in Boston three nights in a row, on his tour behind *Oh Mercy*, his first unembarrassing album since *Blood on the Tracks*. The three shows couldn't have been more different. The first night was astounding. His phrasing was direct and seemed connected to the songs; his band was able to anticipate every barbed cue; even the song he played from the mostly lousy *Shot of Love* sounded spirited. The second night was a disaster, the sound of someone too disconnected to open his mouth wide enough to sing or listen to or care about what he was doing. The third night was mediocre, professional, adequate, not terrible, but boring. Granted, I should have called it quits after the first night, but over the three nights I heard the breadth of what Dylan had to offer. (Jason and the Scorchers opened all three nights and were tremendous.)

A Dylan concert was always a surprise, albeit not always a welcome surprise. If Springsteen had called on Dylan to join him the night before at Shea, the collaboration might have been transcendent. It might have been just OK. Unless you were able to get inside Dylan's head (not recommended), there was no way to know. But you knew Springsteen and the E Street Band would play hard, play tough, play straight, no matter what. And that's what makes Springsteen's shadow something so hard to shake. There are performers who can reach Springsteen's heights some time, but there's no one who can be so damn good almost every time. In his shows and records, Springsteen stands for hard work every time out and almost every night he and his band live up to it. It's an almost impossible standard to meet. No wonder everyone from John Mellencamp to every anonymous bar-band bassist on the Jersey shore finds it frustrating. How can you not find yourself stuck in the shadow of something like that?

Chapter 2

Side Two

I'm a nut about Marcel Proust. I have lived through his big, fat novel in three translations (Scott Moncrieff, Kilmartin-to-Enright, and the recent everyone-gets-a-different-volume-to-translate set from Penguin), as well as too many books about the man, his work, and his housekeeper than I care to enumerate here. When you're so deep into an artist's work, it's easy to start thinking that the work, which seems to be so all-encompassing, can actually answer questions about your real life. Alain de Botton's witty and erudite *How Proust Can Change Your Life* takes a crack at what *In Search of Lost Time* might say to you and me. Each of its chapters is titled "How To" something or other. Its last chapter, though, is titled "How To Put Books Down." The last sentence of his book: "Even the finest books deserve to be tossed aside."

It's hard not to think of this aphorism when considering the impact Bruce Springsteen's work has had on thousands of his fans, because completists, the people who can't toss anything aside, are crazy people. You know them: the folks who can tell you why the alternate mono take on the Ukrainian B-side is superior to the one on the Belarusian eight-track that's three seconds shorter. Sometimes they're inspired crazy people, like Dean Blackwood, the auteur behind Revenant Records, the man behind the box set *Screamin' and Hollerin' the Blues: The Worlds of Charley Patton*, perhaps the most obsessively beautiful package of the CD age, who once told me he felt his relationship to some pieces of vintage 78-rpm vinyl was "borderline fetishistic." Sometimes they're crazy people like the narrator of Richard Thompson's "Don't Sit on My Jimmy Shands," whose fear that someone might hurt his beloved antique vinyl prevents him from having anything resembling a life. Fans have a right to be grateful to labels like Blackwood's Revenant, Michael Cuscuna's Mosaic, and Richard Weize's Bear Family, who will take everything by a beloved performer, including material you never knew existed, material the performer in question might not remember, and wrap it up in an elaborate container.

To a degree, anyway. The problem, of course, is that no artist, not even your favorite one, deserves the completist treatment. If you have a fast Internet connection and deep pockets, you can download a 446-cut *Com-

plete U2 from the iTunes Music Store for a mere $149, but you're filling a database rather than initiating a pleasant listening experience. U2 is a pretty good band (preferable in rockers' garb to earnest mode), but even Bono at his most self-obsessed would have to admit that 14 different versions of "Discotheque," 12 of "Lemon," 11 of "Mysterious Ways," nine of "I Will Follow," seven of "Mofo," and (OK, you get the point) is way too much for the average bear. The job of sifting the prime stuff from the not-for-the-ages should be the job of the producer or the editor, not the poor sucker who buys the weighty product. There are two boxes celebrating Little Richard's brief but fruitful tenure at Specialty. One runs three CDs and includes at least one version of every song he cut at Specialty. Most of those songs are pretty wonderful, so the set flows nicely. The other is six CDs and doesn't include any extra songs not on the three-CD version, just additional alternate takes of the same songs, some so similar that Richard himself would be hard-pressed to tell them apart. The six-CD model is recommended only to masochists, very lonely people, or writers of pop music books.

This completist nonsense doesn't just happen to music lovers. Consider the Library of America series of books, which are more interested in capturing a famed writer's every burp between its covers than offering readers an optimum experience. There are many volumes in the series like the one devoted to Wallace Stevens that don't differentiate between the poet's juvenilia and his masterworks. The message: Everything here is important because it's all by him.

No! There is a difference between a great artist's best works and his or her subpar efforts. No one bats 1.000. Even fans of giants such as Charlie Parker, John Coltrane, and Jimi Hendrix who have waded through record after record of posthumous releases (it seems as if death has made those three men only more prolific) must admit that not everything by a performer deserves to be released. Sometimes a track deserves to remain in a vault. Sometimes a track is unreleased not because it reveals some mystery, but because it's not as good as what did come out.

Until Bruce Springsteen released *Tracks* ('98), a four-CD collection taking in 26 years of mostly unreleased recordings, it was commonly asserted by those who thought they were in the know that his best work was squirreled away in some vault. Because Springsteen has had the misfortune to have many of his studio outtakes heavily bootlegged, the cognoscenti have been able to foster the myth of great lost tracks. But when *Tracks* emerged, that wasn't the story it told. There were some marvelous individual cuts on the collection—at least half of its 66 entries were strong enough to have earned a place on an officially released album—but with few exceptions, the songs didn't fit in with the story Springsteen was trying to tell on a particular album. For example, the romantic ballad "Hearts of Stone," wisely passed off to Southside Johnny and the

Asbury Jukes, wouldn't have made sense on the album for which it was recorded, *Darkness on the Edge of Town*, an album on which the narrators, if they feel romantic at all, tend to feel more romantic about automobiles than women. The description of the car in "Racing in the Street" is more detailed and devoted than that of the narrator's lover.

Yet the myth persists. For years, "Murder Incorporated," a *Born in the U.S.A.* outtake, was said to be Springsteen's Great Lost Song. After it saw the light of day on the '95 *Greatest Hits*, "My Love Will Not Let You Down," another song left off *Born in the U.S.A.*, received the honor. After that showed up on *Tracks*, the title went to "County Fair," which appeared subsequently on the *Essential* bonus disc in '03. Now maybe it's "Chevrolet Deluxe"; after that comes out, it'll be something else ("Cindy"?). Sometimes fans, especially knowledgeable ones, like to think they know better than the artist. It makes good argument fodder: How would you have sequenced this record? What would you have left off? And what of the many unreleased songs we don't even know exist? It's fun, but it's a particularly fruitless exercise when undertaken in regard to Springsteen, a performer legendary (and, to some, legendarily infuriating) for keeping these decisions close to the vest. If the songs didn't come out, there are likely good reasons. And it's his decision, not ours.

I had to learn that the hard way. An early, much longer draft of this chapter (which, honestly, you're

49

lucky not to be reading) played that If-Only-You-Could-Hear-It game. It burrowed through the music Springsteen made before he signed with Columbia in '72, in great detail. (It had to be great detail, because I had to assume that few readers had access to the music in question.) But then I realized that approach was unfair. The music of units like the Rogues, the Castiles, Steel Mill, Dr. Zoom and the Sonic Boom, and the first Bruce Springsteen Band may be cherished by diehard fans with an addiction to BitTorrent, but it's marginal, juvenilia, early work of a soon-to-be-but-not-yet-major-artist that sheds little light on what makes him great. You can hear bits and pieces of the beginnings of his singing and guitar style, but not much of the songwriter he would become. He never played any of these early songs after signing his major-label deal, aside from an occasional "You Mean So Much to Me" (like so many others, passed on to the grateful Southside Johnny, who recorded the definitive version as a revved-up duet with Ronnie Spector). The more I listened to them, the more I realized the songs are not important to any under-standing of Springsteen's subsequent work. (Neither are a pair of brief pieces he wrote for *Seascape*, a student publication, during his brief and apparently fruitless tenure as a student at Ocean County Community Col-lege. You can find them at museums.) Springsteen never plays these songs, he never talks about these songs, he never uses them as source material. Unfortunately, I had to devote many hours listening to that music before I came to that conclusion. But, in the spirit of reissue producers who whittle down 50 hours of archives into one or two CDs of what is worth listening to, I listened to it so you don't have to! You want to listen to an important performer? Listen to him when he starts to do something important. Listen to what he does in the first verse of "Blinded by the Light," the kickoff song of Springsteen's first record, *Greetings from Asbury Park, N.J.* Its landslide of hilarious, frankly Dylanesque lines couldn't have come at a better time. Early '73, when Columbia released the debut, was a quiet time for Dylan fans, who hadn't heard a new LP from their hero since '70, and no one would argue that the low-key *New Morning*, a salvage job from a failed collaboration with Archibald MacLeish, approximated the amphetaminiac glory of his best mid-sixties work. (The disaster *Self-Portrait*, which came out several months before *New Morning*, was conveniently forgotten already.) Springsteen's torrent of words sounded like the Dylan of "115th Dream," someone who loved words so much he could barely contain his delight and laughter at what they could do.

In its five minutes and three seconds, all giddy internal rhymes and words whose power arose from the fact that they didn't make much (any?) literal sense, "Blinded by the Light" gave listeners entry into one uniquely barbed mind. One character in the song is a "brimstone baritone anti-cyclone rolling stone preacher from the east," who advises his followers to "Dethrone the Dictaphone." In the context of these lyrics, it sounds like sage counsel. Meanwhile, an "avatar" recommends that his audience "blow the bar but first remove the cookie jar we're gonna teach those boys to laugh too soon." Thanks for the advice.

The words of "Blinded by the Light" promised entry to a weird, wonderful world in which making literal sense might not be all that important. Indeed, it might be an impediment. The words were high-quality Dylan, I suppose, better than the master himself (a labelmate, it turned out: Springsteen, like Dylan, was signed to Columbia by John Hammond) was issuing those days. At the very least, the song shot Springsteen immediately to the top of the pile of New Dylans, a fact made clear when Manfred Mann, who at the time was specializing in Dylan covers, twisted "Blinded by the Light" to his own opaque purposes, all the way up the pop charts (literally all the way: In early '77 it became what is still the only Springsteen composition to become a *Billboard* Number One single). But the funky music Springsteen wrote and performed for "Blinded by the Light" was not Dylanesque in the least. Its layered guitars—chunky rhythm and spry lead—led a King Curtis–tinged saxophone and a melodic bass (overdubbed by Springsteen himself), along with a drummer who seemed to have trouble concentrating on one song at a time, and all that was before the singer opened his mouth. All of the New Dylans before (and since) Springsteen wanted their words to sound as wild as Dylan's. Springsteen was different. He wanted what all the New Dylans wanted—Dylan-quality words—but he wanted music as wild as Dylan's at its peak and—here's the important part—music that didn't sound like Dylan. What Springsteen got from Dylan was more an invitation to go deep into his own imagination than merely borrow a subset of Dylan's imagination. Like Dylan, Springsteen certainly had folkie leanings—it was during his year performing solo, after the better part of a decade in bands, that he had finally written songs that were worthy of major-label interest—but he was also a rock'n'roller at heart. *Greetings from Asbury Park, N.J.*, was a record for which Springsteen wrote the lyrics first and then built music around the words, the only album he constructed using that method, most of it written, as Springsteen once recalled, "in the back of a closed beauty salon on the floor beneath my apartment in Asbury Park." Not until the monochromatic *The Ghost of Tom Joad* ('95) would he again record an album in which the words were more important than the music. But the music was no afterthought. His desire for exciting settings was Dylan-inspired, not Dylanesque. Dylan could tune up rowdy, weird music that made listeners laugh like they did at his words ("Highway 61 Revisited," "Rainy Day Women #12 and #35"). Springsteen picked up the method, though he didn't follow Dylan's specific instructions. He learned from Dylan how to be free musically as well as lyrically, not what to do specifically. Dylan's records gave Springsteen more inspiration than guidance.

"Blinded by the Light" launches *Greetings* with one of its most assured vocal performances. Springsteen's singing—light but authoritative, wry but sincere—and the background vocals on the choruses (which sound like overdubbed Bruce more than his studio mates) provides a warm, friendly overture for the record. And, in dramatic fashion, the best part of the song comes at the end. After a dizzying array of images, an avalanche of digressions, in its final couplet "Blinded by the Light" gets around to the point of the song: "Mama always told me not to look into the sights of the sun/Oh but mama that's where the fun is." This debut album will be the story of a wise young man ignoring good advice and winding up the better for it. Indeed, the six lasting songs here ("Blinded," plus "Growin' Up," "Does This Bus Stop at 82nd Street?", "For You," "Spirit in the Night," and "It's Hard to Be a Saint in the City") share a romanticism and an affection that are missing in the three cuts that don't work: "Mary Queen of Arkansas" and "The Angel" are too solemn to connect and "Lost in the Flood," a postapocalyptic tale, is put across in a spirited manner. Maybe too spirited. The performance's key moment is the sound of an amplifier head being punched (the perpetrator is The Artist Later To Be Known as Little Steven), perhaps the only genuinely dramatic and ominous moment in a song that tries way too hard to be dramatic and ominous. "Lost in the Flood" even includes the clichéd drop-every-instrument-but-Bruce's-voice gimmick that will return

54

30 years later (even more awkwardly) in "The Fuse." (With any luck, it will be another 30 years before we confront it again on a Springsteen album.) Pop-music historians with too much time on their hands might trace the lyric "Nuns run bald through Vatican halls pregnant pleading immaculate conception" forward to a more vulgar (and more apt) line in the Clash's "Death or Glory" ("I believe in this and it's been tested by research/That he who fucks nuns will later join the Church"), but that doesn't mean Springsteen's line is anything but awkward.

It's strange the awkward line doesn't work, because so much of *Greetings* celebrates awkwardness. The bildungsroman "Growin' Up" has its budding protagonist falling down, throwing up, spending "month-long vacations in the stratosphere"; the even more generous "Does This Bus Stop at 82nd Street?" finds the narrator blessing bus drivers, lovers taking out a "full-page ad in the trades," and a woman who gains fame by pronouncing her belief in hope to the tabloid press. What has lasted longest about *Greetings from Asbury Park, N.J.*, more than 30 years after its release, is not the power of its individual songs—although many exert great power—but the overall feel of friendliness, the transparent excitement Springsteen feels at the possibility of a Big Audience, the determination to squeeze in everything he can and make it count. Even the happiest songs on the record are anything but relaxed. It's a record made by someone who is ready

for his close-up. And when the songs call for Springsteen to be dramatic, he usually delivers. Listen to the
escalating final verse of "For You," the Stagger Lee
evocation that grounds "It's Hard to Be a Saint in the
City," and the farewell to youth on the shores of
Greasy Lake in "Spirit in the Night." Even before he
mastered performing and leading a band in the studio,
he had learned how to structure songs he had first performed solo for a band.

Springsteen gave what seemed like 100 nearly iden-
tical interviews when *Tracks* came out in '98, and in
most of them he would discuss the beginning of his
Columbia recording career, in particular the solo
demos for John Hammond that opened the set: "Mary
Queen of Arkansas," "It's Hard To Be a Saint in the
City," "Growin' Up," and "Does This Bus Stop at
82nd Street?" Looking back, he'd say he now thinks he
should have released those songs in these unadorned
versions. As he told Mark Hagen of *Mojo* in '99, "Listening back now, that pure, very straightforward presentation of those initial songs sounds a little truer to
me now [than the *Greetings* versions]." That's hind-
sight talking. At the time, Springsteen was being tugged
in two directions, and it wasn't entirely clear at the
time who should be pulling where. Hammond wanted
him to be a folkie. Producers Mike Appel and Jim
Cretecos (Appel served double duty as Springsteen's
manager) were eager to show Springsteen around the
studio, but their production style was vague, not push-

ing their client toward his folkie or rock'n'roll sides. And Springsteen was trying to have it both ways, from straight folk like "Mary Queen of Arkansas" to more rocking material like "It's Hard To Be a Saint in the City." When Columbia executive Clive Davis heard the first version of the album, he sent it back to Springsteen and his producers, saying there was nothing on it that could ever be played on commercial radio. Springsteen responded by recalling his band, adding saxophonist Clarence Clemons, and recording "Blinded by the Light" and "Spirit in the Night," completing the record and making it fit for public consumption. Springsteen turned more toward full-band rock'n'roll when challenged to by his label. He could have said he wanted a purer folkie feel to the record and Hammond would have backed him. But that's not what he decided to do. He decided, when pushed, to try and make a hit record. Just as Springsteen fans are often wrong when second-guessing Springsteen, so is the artist himself when he says the record should have been done differently. A *Greetings* without either of those two songs would have been a lesser record and would have gotten less attention from both professionals (critics, disc jockeys) and fans.

You don't have to take my word for it. Easily found on the Internet and specialty shops is a black-and-white video Columbia shot of Springsteen performing solo in August or September '72 (the month varies in memories and published accounts), at Max's Kansas City. It's unclear how much of Springsteen's set was recorded, but two performances survived: "Henry Boy," which didn't make it onto the first record and remains unreleased, and "Growin' Up," which became a staple of the E Street Band's live act for years. Wearing a rolled-up denim shirt, a crucifix hanging around his neck, Springsteen performs tentatively. He's committed, he cares about his material, but his commitment doesn't feel contagious. He introduces "Henry Boy" as being "a song about being new in town," and he sounds nervous. It enjoyed some melodic similarities to "For You" and "Blinded by the Light," but it was nowhere near as distinctive as either. Next up, he intro'd "Growin' Up" as "a song about becoming a man, could be a song about becoming a woman, too, I don't know." Only a notch above mumbling, Springsteen had not yet figured out how to talk to an audience. Words alone were not going to carry him to where he wanted to go. He needed music as strong as his words. "Blinded by the Light" and "Spirit in the Night" gave him that.

Compare that two-song performance with another, longer one that has made the rounds, recorded at the Main Point in Bryn Mawr, Pennsylvania, on April 24, '73, with a full band. At first, what's remarkable is how quiet the band can be, even when they're all playing together. The set is a mix of folk tunes like "Wild Billy's Circus Story," flat-out rockers like "Does This Bus Stop at 82nd Street?" and "Thundercrack," and the sort of extended shaggy-dog tales he was starting to play live that would make his reputation and move him toward the style of his second album. He still speaks slowly and hesitantly, but his forward-looking set (only two of the seven songs were from the already released *Greetings from Asbury Park, N.J.*) was the sound of a band coming together. Several of the new songs were lengthy and episodic, comfortable settings for exploration and experimentation.

But at least that night at the Main Point, Springsteen and his band were playing to his own audience—small, but his own. He didn't always get that chance in '73. Having recorded such a sterling debut as *Greetings from Asbury Park, N.J.*, Columbia promptly decided that the smartest thing for Springsteen to do was concoct a promotional plan that smacked of fakery and send Springsteen on the road as the opening band for the flatulent jazz-rock outfit Chicago. Springsteen remembers the members of Chicago as being kind and warm to him, but the audience was neither and the experience ended, mercifully, after a dozen shows.

As a piece of commercial product, *Greetings from Asbury Park, N.J.*, was a stiff (it didn't even chart until '75, as the *Born to Run* juggernaut began). Airplay was limited to FM rock stations in only a handful of markets, the New Dylan millstone hung heavily around Springsteen's neck (turning off some prominent journalists and disc jockeys, attracting other tastemaker fans), and other Columbia performers were getting the internal attention. The band was gaining confidence every night and Springsteen's new songs held leaps in quality, tenacity, and complexity, but the Columbia Recording Artist did not have a Columbia-sized audience. Money was tight. So Springsteen and his now road-tested E Street Band returned to 914 Sound Studios, a converted-garage studio in Blauvelt, New York, to record an album, released in the fall as *The Wild, the Innocent, and the E Street Shuffle.*

It should have been a disaster. Let's list the ingredients, each of which fed on the previous one:

- The new songs were lengthy, wordy, and intricate. Most of them made the wordplay of "Blinded by the Light," a mere 5:03, seem economical in comparison.
- Even if the song structure was tighter, Springsteen's musical settings were expanding, taking in more chunks of jazz, blues, R&B, and even classical, but producers Appel and Cretecos didn't have any experience in or feel for these styles.
- Even if Appel and Cretecos could give Springsteen direction, the studio at which they chose to record, 914 Sound in Blauvelt, bore the same relationship to a professional studio as a child's scale model of a Corvette does to a real, live gas guzzler. You can imagine they have more in common than they do, but it's all in your head.
- Even if they had chosen to make the album in a professional studio, drummer Vini Lopez, whose

60

role was crucial in a band whose sound was becoming more and more based on groove, was a distraction. His elementary timekeeping skills were limited, and his desire to show off whenever given the briefest opening—why settle for one well-placed snare smack when you can instead hit randomly every drum and cymbal in your kit?—made it impossible for Springsteen to use the drums as a rhythm instrument. It sounded like Lopez wanted to play lead all the time, but he was no Keith Moon.

This is what Springsteen faced as he entered the studio: long songs, wrong studio, indifferent production team, incompatible drummer. Yet in that studio, under those circumstances, he cut his first great album. *The Wild, the Innocent, and the E Street Shuffle* is stuffed not merely with seven classic songs, but with dense, tough-minded but romantic compositions and performances that reveal new surprises, mysteries, and pleasures after hundreds of listenings. (I can vouch for that last part of the assertion personally.) How did he do it?

First, he had to figure out the story he wanted to tell on the record, and that meant jettisoning some fine songs that simply didn't fit. "The Fever," "Santa Ana," "Zero and Blind Terry," "Seaside Bar Song," and "Thundercrack" could have formed the core of a strong record. "Funky epics," Springsteen would later characterize them, and all of them would be released as part of *Tracks* (or, in the case of "The Fever," as one of only three reasons to buy the subsequent ripoff/sampler *18 Tracks*). As a group, they capture a moment in Springsteen's development as a writer and performer. "The Fever" is a slow, swinging soul ballad, one in which Springsteen takes advantage of the sonic limitations of 914 Sound by creating something that sounds like Ray Charles about five minutes after the invention of electricity. It coheres, but it's loose. And *loose* was the watchword of the time. In songs like "Santa Ana" and "Zero and Blind Terry," you can hear Springsteen find ways to marry his love for stuffing as many words as possible into each song and still have a song with a groove. It's the kind of storytelling that works best when put across by a friendly, danceable band. One night at a club in Pennsylvania, Springsteen introduced "Santa Ana" by telling a story of a south-of-the-border trip he and his father took to Tijuana and then reveals the process by which he was able to turn it into a song: "I was able to shrug off the reality of the situation." Those shows were full of half-serious musical experimentation. For a time you could hear "Spirit in the Night" with a harmonica, or a slurry, cosmically funky version of Rufus Thomas's "Walking the Dog" with a police whistle. (Some of the songs the band played live around that time, like "Bishop Danced" and "Tokyo," were just too weird to consider for inclusion on a major-label record.) Most nights in '73, Springsteen would end the set with "Thundercrack." Although it's heard now as a precursor to "Rosalita (Come Out Tonight)"—a theory that gains credence when you remember that the band stopped playing "Thundercrack" as soon as Rosie came out—"Thundercrack" is a more peculiar number, all starts and stops, nonsensical lyrics, populated by outlandish sections that have no right to have anything to say to the other sections, but they do. Even better—and one of the rejected songs that could have earned a spot on *The Wild, the Innocent, and the E Street Shuffle*—was the brief, organ-driven, self-explanatory "Seaside Bar Song." It offered enormous fun and release, but it was one-dimensional and would have been the eighth-best song on an eight-cut LP. And '73 was not the era of 77-minute, CD-length, albums, so Springsteen chose the seven best songs that would fit on a limited slab of vinyl.

But what did fit? What was the winding story Bruce Springsteen wanted to tell on *The Wild, the Innocent, and the E Street Shuffle?* To start with, he wanted to tell a story with a band. Although he's never shared billing with the E Street Band (before or after) on any of his studio records (he saves that for live recordings), Springsteen intended his second album to be the romanticized story of a community, and his band was intended to stand in for that community. It's why they're pictured on the back cover of the LP; it's why the first song of the album gives both the album and the band their names. The record imagines a world in which everyone has a nickname (characters in the songs, band members, everyone) and everyone from crooks to prostitutes, unfaithful lovers to disapproving parents, are invited to the party.

It's also a record about two disparate universes: New Jersey and New York. The songs talk to each other across the huge gap between the two. For "Jungleland," one of the songs he would write while on "tour" behind *The Wild, the Innocent, and the E Street Shuffle*, Springsteen created a character who "drove his sleek machine over the Jersey state line" into New York. That ease of passage is nowhere to be heard on this record, though. The romanticized midnight Manhattan of "Incident on 57th Street" and "New York City Serenade" echo one another, worlds apart from the decaying Jersey shore of "4th of July, Asbury Park (Sandy)" and "Rosalita (Come Out Tonight)." "Kitty's Back" delineates the distance between the two worlds separated by the Hudson, "Wild Billy's Circus Story" promises escape beyond those two poles, and "The E Street Shuffle" (as well as "Kitty's Back") shines a light on how much you might miss if you do leave home. Throughout the record, written from the New Jersey point of view, is the feeling that New York is an infinitely more exciting place to be. As the record ends, with Springsteen charmed by the early-morning sound of a Manhattan trash collector singing, it's easy to imagine him walking down to the Port Authority Bus Terminal, ready to slump in a waiting room, waiting for the first bus of the next day to take him back home to Jersey.

He's picked mostly good company for the journeys there and back. Saxophonist Clemons, drummer Lopez, and bassist Garry Tallent return from the *Greetings* debut, and Springsteen's decision to plug in his electric guitar more often makes the ride more fun. More important, the newer band makes room for the twin keyboards of Danny Federici and David Sancious, two players with different, complementary approaches. It's too simple to call Federici, who plays mostly organ and accordion and played with Springsteen first (even though Sancious played on *Greetings* and Federici didn't), the more emotional player and pianist Sancious the more studied of the pair, but that does broadly spell out their musical roles. Federici has great technical aptitude and Sancious's playing has great soul, and they do spend a good amount of time finishing each other's sentences.

The band leans into the first song on the record, "The E Street Shuffle," caught mid-tuneup, in a brief and funny blast that feels like a New Orleans funeral march played by a group of people who had yet to learn how to play their instruments (indeed, that may have been exactly what was going on). Then the song proper begins and it's immediately apparent how this unit has developed since *Greetings from Asbury Park, N.J.* It's easy to compare right away because the opening guitar lick is a cousin to that of "Blinded by the

Light"; both records start with a blast of rhythm and energy. But there's more going on here. A funky rhythm-guitar line shadowboxing in the background could have fit on Shuggy Otis's "Strawberry Letter 23" and all the guitar effects are denser. From the first line—"Sparks fly on E Street when the boy prophets walk it handsome and hot"—it's clear how Springsteen's singing has opened up and how he has grown as a bandleader. In particular, he's calling on more sources than his beloved mid-sixties Bobby Zimmerman: By the end of the first verse you can hear a bit of Booker T. and the MGs, a touch of Muscle Shoals, some more Major Lance, and most of all Van Morrison. Although the words are wackier than anything Morrison would want to release, Van is everywhere here: in the vocal excitement, in the horn lines, in the "Wild Night" rhythms. The mood is loose, exuberant, the soundtrack to a party. "The E Street Shuffle," after all, isn't merely the title of a song—it's the name of a dance. When you hear the band members chant "everybody form a line!" on the chorus, they're shouting with such bliss that the words sound more like description than an imperative. The song peaks on Springsteen's wordless cry, scraping past the top of his vocal range, capping a soul party that he presides over with a wraparound smile. And that's not the end of the story: After a false ending, the band comes right back in, introducing new riffs and rhythms, having so much fun they can't end it yet.

"The E Street Shuffle" has had a curious history onstage. Although built for live performance, it was only briefly a regular part of the band's live set, sometimes in a slow, piano-led version that flowed from a made-up story Springsteen would tell about having met Clarence in some bad weather/supernatural circumstance on the boardwalk at Asbury Park. It was spirited enough, but far more relaxed and smooth than the one-step-away-from-out-of-control version on *The Wild, the Innocent, and the E Street Shuffle*. Springsteen retired the song after his '78 tour, and didn't return to it until one Saturday night in June '00, at Madison Square Garden, on the last stop of a long tour. He played it again several nights later, during the last performance of the tour, and that version exists, in audio version only, playing over the credits at the end of the second disc of the *Live in New York City* collection. It should be the definitive version: That DVD captures the reunited E Street Band at the height of their powers, Max Weinberg is an infinitely more interesting drummer than Vini Lopez, and it was a welcome blast of happiness during a particularly intense set: The song of the moment, "American Skin (41 Shots)," had made the Manhattan homecoming shows surprisingly confrontational. Anyway, the song as played that night was stripped down from the studio take, with no horn introduction or return after a false ending (pretty good sax solo, though). Springsteen announced the song a bit sheepishly that night ("we've never played this one before") and despite the many smiles onstage—particularly from the band members who played on the original—something was missing. At Madison Square Garden, with all the right pieces in place, we heard a professional rock-'n'roll band play a very good version of a very good song. But on *The Wild, The Innocent, and the E Street Shuffle*, we hear something different, and more revealing and unrepeatable: the sound of a band literally coming together. For someone whose sophomore record had to introduce him to an audience who missed him the first time around, Springsteen couldn't have asked for a better second chance at a first impression.

Both of Springsteen's '73 albums are about place: the title of the first cites his adopted hometown (he grew up in inland Freehold), while the title of the second includes a street from that area (pianist Sancious lived either on or near—again, memories differ—E Street at the time). "4th of July, Asbury Park (Sandy)" is a snapshot from home. It's another acoustic-based ballad. It might sound at first like it could fit in with the sometimes underproduced performances of the debut, but the overdubbed electric guitars in the first verse swiftly add character and share the load. A melodic bass, saxophone, and accordion nail the song to the boardwalk Springsteen sings about. "4th of July, Asbury Park (Sandy)" is yet another song that revels in the narrator's failure. By the end of the song, he's gotten stuck on a carnival ride, been fired and dumped, and can't even deliver the line intended to talk Sandy into bed—"I promise I'll love you forever"—without insert-ing a question mark into the pledge. The key lyric, deployed right before the final chorus, is the defiant "For me this boardwalk life is through/You ought to quit this scene, too," but there's no indication this guy is going anywhere. He sounds far, far away from the narrator of "Thunder Road" (from *Born to Run*, '75) who ends a similar attempt at wooing by proclaiming "It's a town full of losers/I'm pullin' out here to win" and then hitting the road. The two songs have some-thing in common: They're both about the narrator and we never get much of a sense of who Sandy and Mary are, except as projections of the singer's desires. But the singers are moving in different directions. Only one might be bound for anything resembling glory. The other will be consulting Madame Marie for advice for a long time.

"4th of July, Asbury Park (Sandy)," a warm tale of failure, is a musical success that tells one of the simplest stories on *The Wild, The Innocent, and the E Street Shuffle*, yet the arrangement is quite complex, instru-ments and voices weaving in and out of the mix like arcade-videogame characters. The song can take this weight because Springsteen is taking such bizarre chances in the studio. A children's chorus was planned for the background vocals. That didn't work out, so Suki Lahav, wife of the record's engineer Louis Lahav and a formidable violin player and singer, repeatedly overdubbed her ethereal voice until she sounded like a children's chorus. The chances are more frequent and more dizzying in "Kitty's Back," another song about romantic loss and (maybe) return, this time put across with jazzy joy. "Kitty's Back," like "The E Street Shuffle" and "Rosalita (Come Out Tonight)," is built for live performance, intended to make those who've never heard the band before take notice (and those who *have* heard the band go nuts). The E Street Band had plenty of chances to convince new ears, opening shows for everyone from Chicago to Chuck Berry (an experience Springsteen retells in the Berry documentary film *Hail, Hail Rock'n'Roll*) to Blood, Sweat & Tears to Anne Murray. Murray fans in particular were likely to have been surprised by "Kitty's Back," which is almost antithetical to "Snowbird" fare. It charges out of the gate with a blues-drenched electric guitar, Tallent's bass buried in the mix but providing a strong counterweight, linking the guitar to the beat. (Unlike "The E Street Shuffle," the beat here is a bona fide shuffle.) The story of the lyrics isn't anything new—girl leaves boy and heads Uptown, boy is sad, girl comes back—but this is the song on *The Wild, The Innocent, and the E Street Shuffle* that leaves *Greetings from Asbury Park, N.J.* behind: It's all about the music. The instrumental section in the middle was meant to make crowds go crazy: solo after solo, each dragging the song higher and higher, first organ, then guitar (at least two of them, maybe three, overdubbed onto each other like stacks of hot pancakes), then horns and organ and guitar all butting heads, cracking up while they fight for space. Springsteen was the acknowledged leader, but "Kitty's Back" showcased a band that was very much alive in its interplay. The excitement in the band when Kitty returns, Springsteen whispering in surprise, "Here she comes," is as joyous as any rock'n'roll sound you can come up with. And the fact that her return is ambivalent makes it something worth thinking about as well as dancing to.

It's easy to think that the escape from New Jersey promised in "Wild Billy's Circus Story" might end up the same way as Kitty's, as the first half of an inevitable round trip. The song has a *Greetings* feel, though the tuba and accordion bring us back to the boardwalk. (The overdubbed harmonica signals that Springsteen is focused on full-blown record-making now, not capturing a straight coffeehouse vibe in the studio.) As a lyricist, Springsteen tries for more realistic details, but he can't stop with barbed romantic images like "the man-beast lies in his cage sniffin' popcorn." The couplet at the end of the song—"Hey son, you wanna try the Big Top?/All aboard, Nebraska's our next stop"—is directed by the circus boss toward a new recruit, at least it is literally, but it's also an invitation from Springsteen to his (mostly imagined at this point) audience. Compared to what is happening with his peers in Freehold and Asbury Park, the folks most likely to witness an E Street Band performance, Springsteen has run off and started his own circus. Why not join him?

71

And that's just the first side. Flip the record and you're confronted by a three-piece suite—"Incident on 57th Street," "Rosalita (Come Out Tonight)," and "New York City Serenade"—that adds up to one of the most successful (and one of the least pretentious) linked sides since rock'n'roll started offering up albums as something more than just song after song. In comparison, the second side of the Beatles' *Abbey Road* is merely clever. Ditto for the Beach Boys' *Pet Sounds*. As full-side concepts go, only Van Morrison's *Astral Weeks* (pick either side) surrenders a comparable musical and emotional intensity. (By a conceptual side, I don't mean something literal and overblown like something from Yes or Pink Floyd. Instead, I'm referring to half-albums in which the songs, however great on their own, mean a little less separated from their comrades.) This second side chronicles both sides of the New Jersey/New York divide. It's more romance than class that surrounds the two. Don't write off Side Two as a rock'n'roll version of *Upstairs, Downstairs*; remember that no one in either locale appears to have any money. The two New York songs that start and end the side are slow and deliberate. Shoehorned in the middle, the Jersey story, despite its many musical and lyrical changes, rocks out from beginning to end. Although New York is presented as the place those from New Jersey escape *to*, it sounds like those left behind in area code 201 might be having more fun.

"Incident on 57th Street," with its piano and organ interplay and tale of Manhattan hoods no more successful than the guy in "4th of July, Asbury Park (Sandy)," isn't meant to be realistic. There are no "little barefoot street boys" (punks? criminals?) who "left the corners, threw away all their switchblade knives, and kissed each other goodbye." The references to Romeo and Juliet keep the song a little too close to *West Side Story* and a little too far from the real 57th Street. Spanish Johnny, the song's hero, sits on a fire escape and calls to the kids playing on the street, "Hey little heroes, summer's long but it ain't very sweet around here anymore." Now that's not a sentence anyone has ever said in the history of the planet. But even if people don't ever talk like this, they do feel this way. Side Two of *The Wild, the Innocent, and the E Street Shuffle* is about communicating real feeling using the most heightened romantic tools: Springsteen shrugs off the literal reality of the situation so he can create something that feels more real than mere reporting.

The Wild, the Innocent, and the E Street Shuffle is the only Springsteen record without a lyric sheet. Chances are that happened for financial reasons—sales of *Greetings from Asbury Park, N.J.* couldn't have encouraged Columbia to spring for a typeset inner sleeve—but it does, albeit inadvertently, emphasize that Springsteen, the former New Dylan, wants to get across as a writer and performer of music, not just words. He does as "Incident on 57th Street" builds. The last chorus repeats and repeats and gets louder and deeper and louder and deeper, reaching an almost gospel feeling that bears no relation to gospel form, resolving into a piercing guitar, rolling back and forth between guitar and organ on what feels like a fading coda, but one element remains: Sancious's piano, enjoying the space, giving the rest of the band a moment to catch its collective breath, rising, and then . . .

What comes next is, to these jaded ears, the most exciting segue ever on a rock'n'roll record (the only ones that come close are the links between the two parts of Derek and the Dominos' "Layla" and the Rolling Stones' "Can't You Hear Me Knockin'"). But before we thrill to how the solo piano at the end of "Incident on 57th Street" resolves into the big, bad guitar that throws open the doors to "Rosalita (Come Out Tonight)," let's consider for a moment what Springsteen has been able to do with "Incident on 57th Street" live. He's presented it in a variety of settings: sometimes just him on piano, sometimes with the full band. He hasn't played it regularly since the first leg of the *Born to Run* tour and he rarely plays it as he did during the middle night of a December '80 stand in Uniondale, Long Island, in a late-in-the-set version that segues, as it does on the album, into "Rosalita." Preserved as one of the B-sides associated with the mammoth *Live/1975–85* ('86), this live version serves as the antidote to the *Live in New York City* version of "The E Street Shuffle." On the Long Island "Incident on 57th Street," we can hear why the '73 version of the E Street Band could only carry Springsteen so far. The arrangement remains dense but clear, and it's in the best part of the song, the instrumental break at the end, that the "classic" version of the E Street Band shows its mettle. Springsteen's guitar solo is longer and harder, darting between organ blasts, but it's Max Weinberg's precise, almost martial drumming that lifts the song to something resembling Rock'n'roll Heaven. It's a solid foundation, as hard and as much a lead instrument as something Keith Moon would invent, but it never strays from being a rhythm instrument and tries to take over the song.

At Uniondale's Nassau Coliseum, Weinberg, a clear fan of the song, could do something rare—sit on the drummer's stool for the big segue (even when Springsteen was calling for "Incident on 57th Street" regularly, he usually didn't place it right before "Rosalita" in the set). Drums fall away, piano rises, and—Boom!—it's "Rosalita." More than 30 years after it was recorded, "Rosalita" remains one of the dozen or so songs most closely associated with Springsteen, and he did close his sets with it almost every night he played a concert from '74 to '85. The lyric is simple—I'm going to be a rock'n'roll star, I'm going to transcend my Jerseyness, and you ought to be my girl—but it's put across with so much enthusiasm and surprise that it's as if Springsteen is trying to win the hearts of his audience, not just one lucky young woman. The song is meant to turn heads everywhere. Springsteen later wrote that that song "was my musical autobiography." It was up to that point, but it was also the end of one part of his story. Funny, serious, self-deprecating, boasting (Lopez's abandon fits in more than usual here), snaking through section after section, the song keeps rising and rising, way past where it seems possible, into a world where an observation like "closets are for hangers" can sound offhand-profound. With a story that took you from a car stuck in the mud "somewhere in the swamps of Jersey" to the promise of "a pretty little place in Southern California down San Diego way," "Rosalita" wasn't merely the finest rock'n'roll song Springsteen had recorded so far; it was the funniest. It had . . . everything. You'd end your shows with it too if you had thought of it. More than seven minutes long, the song ends with the sound of six very happy grown men collapsing in a heap. It's no accident that after Springsteen began performing this song live, his performances began to get longer and longer, eventually peaking beyond four hours before reason kicked in and he pulled back. Springsteen played until he was exhausted. He wanted his audience to feel the same way.

At the beginning of "New York City Serenade," it seems as if David Sancious, the man kind enough to lead us from "Incident on 57th Street" to "Rosalita," is the first to work his way back up. (Granted, he doesn't have to stand up, just pull himself up to his piano stool.) His long piano introduction, steeped in classical training, starts weird, turns ominous, then welcome and jazzy, until Springsteen's acoustic guitar snaps into place next to it. Ariel Swartley once wrote (in Greil Marcus's *Stranded* collection) that Springsteen's guitar enters "soft and startling like an unexpected kiss," a description that can't be improved upon. The song is about a Jersey boy walking the romantic streets of late-night-to-early-morning Manhattan, first just observing (the first verse is in third person) and then becoming part of the dreamy chronicle, as the strings push Springsteen to sing harder and deeper, to get more and more involved. He details an alternative "midnight in Manhattan" universe in which everything is forgiven (a theme he'd take all the way to "Land of Hope and Dreams" and parts of *The Rising*), where you can "shake away your street life/shake away your city life." At the end, Springsteen presents an image as unrealistic as it is indelible: a trash collector, dressed in satin, singing, dispensing beauty in the midst of garbage. With Clemons's beautiful saxophone soaring around him, Springsteen marvels at what he hears: "He's singin', singin', singin', singin'." Last record out you could hear the Dylan in him. Half an hour ago it was all Van Morrison. Now, as "New York City Serenade" goes out on a one-note fade, Springsteen has moved past comparison.

Listening to someone singing, gaining strength and solace from it, building a life around it: Once, a long time ago, while I was producing a Sun Records box set, I had the honor of spending a day with Sam Phillips, the genius who, along with folks like Johnny Cash,

Howlin' Wolf, Carl Perkins, Elvis Presley, and Charlie Rich, invented the past 50 years of popular music. Sometimes he tried to intimidate me (he would stare through me without blinking to emphasize a point), sometimes he tried to confuse me (he called John Philip Sousa "my greatest hero"), but most of the time he tried to teach me. "Think about it," he said four hours into a conversation. "Think about the things that are most important in your life. What are they?" I told him about my wife and my child, and he stopped me. "No! That's not it. That's not why you're alive. That's not why you're here. It's music. Music! It's the universal language, just a man beating on the side of a wooden box. There's nothing like it: No painting, no sermon, no book. Nothing. Music is its own distinct master. Nothing makes you feel like music makes you feel. The greatest thing on this earth is being able to feel something! That's the greatest freedom in the world. That's what I wanted my records to make you do. That's all. That's it. You can leave now." He didn't say another word. He didn't have to. Philips, the single most important non-performing figure in rock'n'roll, lived in the same world that Springsteen celebrates at the end of "New York City Serenade," the world in which artists can find fountains in deserts, the world in which nothing can hold back the power of music to change everything about you.

All the ingredients were so wrong. The results were so right. Or: Maybe it was the right studio. Maybe it was the right producers. Maybe it was the right drummer. Maybe *The Wild, the Innocent, and the E Street Shuffle* was made by someone with a vision so pure it could cut through any obstacle.

What happened to this masterpiece in the marketplace? It sold even more anemically than *Greetings*—with an average song length of nearly seven minutes it was hard to cull anything resembling a single—so Springsteen's major-label deal was tenuous at best after *Wild* followed its predecessor and never appeared on the *Billboard* albums chart. Springsteen's records didn't sell, but something was happening in the bars and clubs up and down the Boston-Washington corridor that he toured so tirelessly. Not many attended these shows, although many later claimed they did. If all the people who said they witnessed some legendary early E Street Band shows in Philadelphia were actually there, the band would have been playing the Spectrum, the local arena. Springsteen sought to capture the breadth of rock'n'roll in those shows, from the silly to the profound. Those who did attend these long, personal, unprecedented shows came away with the fervor of the newly converted.

The most important of those attendees was producer and critic Jon Landau, who saw a May 9, '74, E Street Band performance in Cambridge, Massachusetts, that changed his life and, as a result, Springsteen's. In a very personal essay published later that month in Boston's *Real Paper*, Landau wrote of being sick of life, sick of music, and restored by Springsteen's show. In a nod to his own curmudgeoness and Dickens's *Christmas Carol*, he identified Springsteen as "rock and roll future." The label stuck (Columbia milked it until the hype turned sour), it started Springsteen down the road to naming Landau his producer and manager, and it put in print what people attending these shows were feeling. Here was Springsteen, a guy with no hit records, a scary-looking band, and a love for some of the strangest songs you wouldn't associate with a New Anybody (live covers at the time ranged from Fats Domino's "Let the Four Winds Blow" to Lambert, Hendricks, and Ross's "Gimme That Wine"). But he was doing something different. Radio broadcasts up and down the East Coast spread the word (and, after Springsteen did score some hits, supported bootleggers). Heads were turning. This couldn't go on. It had to change.

Another thing that had to change was the band lineup. Drummer Lopez left the band (both personal and musical reasons were cited), replaced by Ernest Carter, a childhood friend of Sancious's, who added a less wiggly anchor to the band. In August, after Sancious got a record deal, Carter left with him, leading Springsteen and Appel to take out this classified ad in the *Village Voice*:

Drummer (no jr. Ginger Bakers, must
Encompass R&B and jazz), pianist
(classical to Jerry Lee Lewis),

Trumpet (must play r&b, Latin & jazz),
violinist. All must sing. Male or
female. Immed auditions for Bruce
Springsteen & the E Street Band
(Columbia Records). Appel. 759-1610
10AM-6PM

This was the ad that brought drummer Max Weinberg and pianist Roy Bittan to the E Street Band. (Suki Lahav, who had sung on the previous album, would stick around for several more months as a singer and violinist.) Weinberg and Bittan both offered a combination of professionalism and spirit that gave the band the sound that made it fill arenas and stadiums. They had the chops to play in Broadway pit bands and the imagination to want to do something more interesting with their talents. Not a bad result for one classified ad.

That's a happy ending to the story, but it's unclear from the ad if that's what Springsteen was looking for. The terms *R&B* and *jazz* appear twice in the ad. And *Latin*? Weinberg and Bittan beefed up the band's sound immeasurably, but not by adding any R&B or jazz to it. The desire for a trumpet player? The brief text in the ad points to a different sound, an attempt to stretch out even more, to get farther away from mainstream rock-'n'roll. That's not where Springsteen decided to go after Bittan and Weinberg had joined the team. The new songs he was writing were more concise, more straight-ahead rockers, and he brought on board the right people to support those songs. The ad hints at what was going on in his mind at the time and where he might have gone, how he might have extended the sound of the first two albums instead of striking out for something new, as he did on *Born to Run*. Before we bid these two albums goodbye and listen to the music Springsteen made that gave him a mass audience and helped him retain it, let's remember that Springsteen's first two albums offer the loosest, funniest, and most eccentric music of his career. Never again would his records sound so free. On September 18, '74, again at the Main Point in Bryn Mawr, Springsteen would debut his new drummer and pianist, and the E Street Band would never sound the same again.

Chapter 3

The Road to Nassau

I f rock'n'roll is an important part of your life, chances are it's taken you to some extremes. Indeed, there are some performers who excel only when they're at the extremes, the far edges. Think of Neil Young, who is at his barbed best when he's being really, really quiet or really, really loud. In the middle, he's boring. It was with good reason that, to paraphrase the man himself, he abandoned the middle of the road for those ditches on either side. The same was true for Kurt Cobain and many others.

But what is extreme? Both Young, in Crazy Horse mode (his wildest configuration), and Cobain enjoyed great commercial success when they plugged in and howled. How extreme can they really be if arenas fill to hear them howl? When one's idiosyncrasies crack the mainstream, they're not so idiosyncratic anymore:

They're popular enough to garner an audience among people for whom rock'n'roll is not an important part of their lives. They inspire Weird Al Yankovic parodies and the like. Onstage with Crazy Horse, casting out and reeling in his deceptively complex tall tales and lengthy, arching, volcanic guitar solos, eyes closed to the world while he stands close to his bandmates and does his little hunkered-over dance, Young gives the impression of being at an extreme himself. He's transported himself and we're lucky enough to listen in. But then he opens his eyes, sees some idiots in the amphitheater tapping a beach ball, and the spell is broken. What's happening before his eyes pales before what was happening in his head when his eyes were shut tight. No wonder Miles Davis literally turned his back on his audience for so many years.

Young enjoyed great popularity at an early age, so he never had to ask himself, "Do I want to be a big rock'n'roll star? It will be far more satisfying financially than sharing a van with six other guys, but how about creatively? What kind of audience do I want?" Springsteen took another path. After years of being the Jersey shore's hottest guitar player (Steel Mill played their bombastic blues-rock to large enough crowds that they would have gotten signed eventually), he turned away from his electric six-string long enough to get signed as a solo artist. His two quickly recorded albums didn't sell much, but the reactions he and his E Street Band were receiving for their live shows suggested they could have great fun onstage, even if cover charges and percentages of the bar didn't add up to anything resembling a living wage. If rock'n'roll was just an art project to Springsteen, he was succeeding. He could take himself to extremes artistically. (Not that "extreme" means anything anymore, if Billy Joel, the king of the middle of the road—except when it comes to his own driving—can write a song called "I Go to Extremes" and not get laughed off the planet.)

If rock'n'roll is a popular art (it is), then saying or thinking something along the lines of "Let's put a lid on it. Let's not try to get past where we are commercially," is a cop-out. It's not only cowardly artistically but it's also condescending to the audience, all but announcing that the folks who pay for the concert tickets and records aren't hip enough to keep up with the performer. It assumes that there's something diminished about a great rock'n'roll band that develops a great rock'n'roll audience. The finest records by the Beatles, the Rolling Stones, Bob Dylan, and the Who were also big hit records. It's not like Dylan somehow shortchanged his talent or pandered to his audience when he "went electric" or "went commercial" or whatever you want to call it: His three records right after he made the bold move—*Bringing It All Back Home, Highway 61 Revisited,* and *Blonde on Blonde*—are inarguably his most lasting, arguably the most impressive 1-2-3 in rock'n'roll. Sure, Elvis Presley, the template for a rock'n'roll star, sold out at some point fairly early on (and again and again and again). But even in '54, long before any money came in, when Elvis, Scotty Moore, and Bill Black tore through an Arthur Crudup blues tune, "That's All Right," under the supervision of Mr. Sam Phillips, they were looking to make music that would connect with an audience. "That's different," Phillips said while they played it back that historic night. "That's a pop song now." Not quite: It resembled nothing on the pop radio stations of the day. What Phillips meant by "pop song" was that this new version wasn't quite country, wasn't quite blues. It was . . . different, but it was something that Phillips immediately sensed would move both blues and country fans. That's why it was a "pop song": It could pop into the minds of many different kinds of people, not some small group in the know. It could make its singer a star.

Bruce Springsteen may have been modest personally as a young man but he wanted to be a rock'n'roll *star*. The tight close-up on the cover of *The Wild, the Innocent, and the E Street Shuffle* was the work of someone comfortable with using a big shot of his face to sell records. (A decade later, he would showcase something else to sell records on the cover of *Born in the U.S.A.*) After Springsteen hired pianist Roy Bittan and Max Weinberg, he had the final pieces of a band that could make him a rock'n'roll star, a band whose talent, commitment, and energy could inspire him to write and perform the songs that would make him one. Between '75 and '80, through many hundreds of concerts that doubled in length to four hours and the protracted, meticulous recording of three albums, Bruce Springsteen and the E Street Band developed into nothing less than the greatest American rock'n'roll band.

Whoa. Them's strong words. Well, what's the point in writing a book about a band if you don't believe something superlative about them? And if Bruce Springsteen and the E Street Band didn't make up the greatest American rock'n'roll band, then who did? Line up, likely contestants.

- **The Allman Brothers Band**. They kept playing, all right, with an intensity and focus that could embarrass the many jam bands they inspired. But where are the songs? The loss of Duane Allman early in their career deprived them not only of his dynamic improvisations but of someone who could help them flesh out a repertoire to match their chops. And a band that shares a guitar player, Warren Haynes, with the Dead is always a bit suspect.
- **The Band**. Two peerless albums, right, *Music from Big Pink* and the one with the cover photo that looked like it was shot before Lincoln was? Then they fell off a cliff, give or take the occasional strong cut or live record. Plus, most of 'em were from Canada, which at press time is still a different country.

- **Booker T. and the MG's.** Strong candidates indeed: soulful, precise, surprising, not an ounce of selfishness in their playing. No singer, though.
- **The Byrds.** They're oft-cited, but if you take away the one distinctive element of their original sound (Roger McGuinn's guitar) and the one song that served it so well ("Eight Miles High"), you're stuck with little more than a pretty good Dylan cover band.
- **Crazy Horse.** Playing with Neil Young, you might have an argument. But except for that first record with Danny Whitten, all their records without Neil at the top of the bill are terribly mannered and free of direction.
- **Creedence Clearwater Revival.** This wasn't a band: It was one astonishingly inspired guy with a really good rhythm section that did exactly what he told them to do. And we all know what happened to the band when Doug Clifford and Stu Cook started writing songs (cue sound of car crash).
- **Elvis, Scotty, and Bill.** If only they had lasted . . .
- **The Pretenders.** They had an American sensibility, thanks to the peerless Ohio native Chrissie Hynde, but great songs about Ohio notwithstanding they were 75 percent British so the judges have no choice but to disqualify.
- **Ramones.** They had as distinctive and original a sound as that of any American rock'n'roll band

and their first four albums just got better and better. But did they ever grow in the 20 years that followed?

- **X.** This was a punk band that did grow and expand despite the songwriters thinking they were poets, but they're docked multiple notches for allying themselves with the creepy Doors veteran Ray Manzarek.

How did the E Street Band capture this title, moving from the obscurity of clubs to a unit that could sell out multiple nights at many arenas? By not going to extremes—except in one way. We'll get to that.

Two concerts: one in a small room with 200 people, the other in a hockey arena with 20,000. The band is pretty much the same, and so are some of the songs. One of those songs in both sets is called "Thunder Road." What sets them apart? For one thing, at the time of the February '75 show at the Main Point in Bryn Mawr, "Thunder Road" hasn't been committed to vinyl. It's not even titled "Thunder Road" yet. According to the set list, it's "Wings for Wheels." The unrecorded song is still taking shape, lyrically and musically. The narrator hasn't even decided who he's singing the song to yet. Tonight it's Angelina, soon it will be Chrissie, eventually Mary would be the ultimate object of the singer's desire. The first verse, just Springsteen's voice over a piano, feels intimate, quiet, close: It's a very small room, the audience is small, packed, and interested enough to listen quietly, actively. The lyric shifts quickly from description to monologue and it's seamless. Springsteen gets away with this because the crowd is hanging on to his story, silently rooting for him. He'd better hope Angelina or Chrissie or Mary is taken by his presentation, too, because some of the words coming out of his mouth seem borrowed from the loser in "4th of July, Asbury Park (Sandy)" from *The Wild, the Innocent, and the E Street Shuffle*. "You ain't a beauty but you're alright" is not one of the world's most compelling come-ons, especially from someone insisting you make up your mind because his car is about to overheat. Sax, organ, and violin circle around one another, coming together at unexpected intervals to support Springsteen, who's still alternating between boasts like how good a guitar player he is and hard truths like "I know you're lonely like me." At the end, when Springsteen's narrator announces he was "born to win" and apparently drives away (alone? with Angelina?), the song abruptly moves to a forced beat. It's a bit too happy too quickly. It's lovely, but the party feels unearned.

Then you witness a performance of "Thunder Road" at Nassau Coliseum in Uniondale, Long Island, in the last hours of '80. Now you're surrounded by 20,000 of your closest friends, not 200. The song was the leadoff track on *Born to Run*, released seven months after the Main Point show. The studio version, more focused and optimistic than the early live tryout, has been a regular part of the band's set for three tours, often in the dramatic spot of the last song before the midset intermission (since '78, the shows have gotten so long that a break had to be built in to hold off exhaustion both onstage and offstage). As the song begins, the piano and harmonica intro is met by a roar of recognition, quickly followed by loud handclapping to keep (rush, actually) the beat before the drums slide in. Springsteen sings only some of the words in the first verse, leaving the crowd to shout most of them, roaring even louder at the sound of its own singing. Perhaps Mary will be more impressed if 20,000 people, not just scrawny Springsteen, point out that despite not being a beauty, hey, she's alright.

Come to think of it, there's a similar roar at the beginning of most songs: For "Hungry Heart," the hit single off the most recent album *The River*, Springsteen simply points the microphone at the crowd, which sings the first verse without any vocal assistance from the stage. If you look around, it's not just the hall that's bigger when you compare this "Thunder Road" to the Main Point take. Both, frankly, are thrilling. But what you heard in '75 was the thrill of discovery: Springsteen discovering a new song, an engaged audience discovering a new performer. Now the thrill, at least for those in the know for some time, is that he's not all ours anymore. There's a romance associated with small clubs, but there's also a pleasure in seeing someone worthy break out of them. It also makes the performer's occasional return to the clubs special, not a sign that he can't fill anything more substantial. When fans feel like they own performers—and when performers don't know how to push back—that's when the heartaches begin. But tonight in Long Island, despite being in what has to be (let's be honest) one of the ugliest large halls on the East Coast, the feeling is all celebration. It's not just because it's New Year's Eve. The band has gotten more popular, not gone Hollywood. The era of Courtney Cox videos, actress/model girlfriends, and stadium sellouts is still years away. Most important: No matter how noble you feel bars are compared to basketball halls, this is muscular music made to fill arenas. "Thunder Road" could sound glorious in a club, but the triumph at the end of the song, highlighted by the duel between Springsteen's guitar and Clemons's saxophone as the two line up on opposite edges of the stage and inch toward one another, is outsized enough (and, frankly, stagy enough) to be understood even in the upper decks.

The same song comes across differently in Nassau Coliseum than it did at the Main Point. The Main Point performance captures the E Street Band in glorious transition. Their new members have been integrated into the unit, making the sound more professional without dampening the energy. And the cover choices are still unexpected, ranging from a light version of the Johnny Rivers hit "Mountain of Love," in which Roy Bittan does his best Jerry Lee Lewis imitation, to a slowed-down take of Bob Dylan's "I Want You," in which the lust of the *Blonde on Blonde* version is replaced by a yearning that was in the words all the time, if not in Dylan's performance. Here, "Wings for Wheels"/"Thunder Road" is one of five songs in contention for the next record that are being aired out. It's easy to argue that the trade of Sancious and Carter for Bittan and Weinberg led to an E Street Band that's more conventional (Broadway pit bands don't suffer weirdoes well), but the power they're directing to E Street stalwarts like "Kitty's Back," paired with the sense of abandon they bring to Chuck Berry's "Back in the U.S.A.," which closes the show, emphasizes that the band hadn't traveled too far uptown. As they work on the new material, particularly "Jungleland," which is moving slowly from its jazzy '74 version to what it would become on *Born to Run*, the arrangement taking shape but a guitar solo where Clemons's trademark sax solo would soon reside, you can hear how fun it is to learn something together.

At Nassau, that era of breakthrough is over. This band has recorded hundreds of songs together, played onstage together hundreds of nights. With only one personnel change from the Main Point (shortly afterward, Suki Lahav left and old friend Steve Van Zandt stepped in as a different kind of onstage foil), they are a comfortable, reliable machine. Whatever toll the familiarity might be taking personally, it's not showing up in the music. When Springsteen calls up rarely performed material like "Held Up Without a Gun" (a B-side never played to a paying audience, before or after) or "In the Midnight Hour" (it is New Year's Eve), the band follows. The shared history seems to encompass anything Springsteen can think of. In a word, this version of the band has peaked. If it went on much longer, this musical familiarity would lead to complacency. That would come, but it hasn't happened yet.

If *The Wild, the Innocent, and the E Street Shuffle* is a record about place, *Born to Run*, the album that sparked the band's '75–'80 glory days, is an album about time. It's not merely the day-in-the-life theme, from the Roy Orbison wake-up call on the radio at the entrance to "Thunder Road" to the almost-first-light devastation at the conclusion of "Jungleland." But where *Tunnel of Love* ('87) and the '92 pair of *Human Touch* and *Lucky Town* are records about the ravages of time, *Born to Run*, the work of a much younger man, is a record about the promise of time, anticipation of what may wait ahead rather than regret about what's in the rear-view mirror. There's plenty of heartbreak, both implicit ("Thunder Road") and explicit ("Backstreets"), but there's way more excitement and anticipation on "Tenth Avenue Freeze-Out," "Night," "She's the One," and most of all "Born to Run," a song whose optimism has seemed to expand and become unquenchable over 30 years of performance. There are even characters on *Born to Run* who shouldn't feel optimistic, but are. We as listeners can hear that the small-change

94

hoods in "Meeting Across the River" are doomed, but the singer sees only the promise of "two grand's practically sitting here in my pocket" and how that money will show his lover—the one who's about to walk out on him—that he's not the loser she thinks he is.

With Ernest Carter still sitting on the drummer's stool, the song "Born to Run" was recorded at 914 Sound, long before the rest of the album was cut at the far more upscale Record Plant in Manhattan, with Jon Landau joining the production team. Early-adopter disc jockeys like Ed Sciaky in Philadelphia and Kid Leo in Cleveland were playing the song, to great response. It must have driven manager Mike Appel and the Columbia brass crazy: Springsteen had his first radio hit, on a song that was unavailable for sale. The flip side of that was that both Springsteen and the people thinking about his career now had evidence that the guy was capable of writing a hit single, giving Springsteen a chance to record a third album despite not selling many records first or second time out.

"Born to Run" showed that Springsteen could take all the twists and turns of showstoppers like "Rosalita," "Thundercrack," and "Kitty's Back" and compress them into a taut song that didn't take 10 minutes to lay out its whole story. Anything old-timers might say was lost in extended improvisation was gained in direct communication. And how much improvisation is there room for in a four-and-one-half minute rock-'n'roll anthem? There were enough musical changes and surprises in "Born to Run" to fill a much longer song—false endings, saxophone and guitar fighting to solo at the same time—but they did it in a compressed context. It was, as Sam Phillips might say, "a pop song now," conceding nothing in its quest to hit the big time.

"Born to Run" is as open as Springsteen's intentions. Because some rock'n'roll songs capture the universal, at first Springsteen was worried that he had inadvertently stolen the song. Keith Richards has said the same thing happened to him after he came up with the riff that powers "(I Can't Get No) Satisfaction." While original, "Born to Run" does have antecedents in Springsteen's catalogue. It's another "pulling out of here to win" piece, an optimistic composition and performance that nonetheless deploys the word *suicide* twice in its first verse. There is plenty of unhappiness to overcome in the song, but it's overtaken by the promise of doing something about it. The characters battle the tedium of day jobs by riding "mansions of glory" at night and promising themselves a richer future somewhere else: "we'll run till we drop, baby we'll never go back"; "we're gonna get to that place where we really wanna go and we'll walk in the sun." There's no evidence that any of these good things will actually happen; there's overwhelming evidence that the singer believes they will and that belief is contagious. Only once does the singer "fess up" and wonder whether what he is looking for exists.

Dave Marsh, among others, has suggested that the line "I wanna know if love is real" is the key to understanding Springsteen's career, that Springsteen's songs document the bottomless vagaries of that quest. In his book *Glory Days*, Marsh also gets Springsteen to agree with him, so it's hard to argue. But argue I will. To these ears, the line of "Born to Run" that says the most about what the rest of Springsteen's career will encompass is its very first: "In the days we sweat it out on the street of a runaway American dream." It's all there, folks. It has the split between the mundane day and the limitless night, the inevitability of work, and the desire for community. (It's "*we* sweat it out," not "*I* sweat it out.") Those last three words—*runaway American dream*—encapsulate both the optimism (the existence of an agreed-upon American dream toward which Springsteen's protagonists hope to run) and the less pleasant reality of a dream gone awry, gone missing, gone out of control. You have to live with both sides. What has run away is an "American dream," not an "Asbury dream." After two albums emphasizing the down home, Springsteen's lens has changed from telephoto to wide-angle. The "highway 9" referenced in the song could be anywhere, not necessarily one particular north-south Jersey shore route. It was located, he hoped, wherever you are.

Springsteen is thinking big throughout the record, gaining power by invoking the big guns. "Born to Run" may have sprung from his brain alone, but "She's the

One" invokes the primordial Bo Diddley beat and "Tenth Avenue Freeze-Out" evokes the classic soul rhythms of Al Jackson and Duck Dunn. Although the spirit of the rhythm section of Booker T's MGs hangs over the song, "Tenth Avenue Freeze-Out" is more notable for the role two E Street Band members play on it. Although it pretends to tell another story of how Clarence "Big Man" Clemons joined the band, in fact it documents the arrival of another band member, guitarist Steve Van Zandt, who joined during the recording of the album, contributing an occasional background vocal and salvaging the horn arrangement to "Tenth Avenue Freeze-Out," singing the individual horn parts to the session players (including the highly regarded Brecker brothers) until the parts swung. Along with the three session horn players on that song was E Streeter Clemons, and "Tenth Avenue Freeze-Out" was where the myth of the Big Man began.

What role does Clarence Clemons play in the E Street Band? *The River* was the last (final?) Springsteen studio record in which his saxophone played a crucial part in the arrangements. Every now and then he'll come up with a solo that reminds you how much power and fervor he can bring to a song either as a sax player ("Dancing in the Dark," "Bobby Jean," "Secret Garden," "Land of Hope and Dreams") or as a singer (his brief turn at the microphone during the reunion-tour standard "If I Should Fall Behind"), but over time his role in the band has become more symbolic than musical. More than 30 years on, Clemons is the member of the E Street Band closest to being an actor onstage, in part because his every gesture earns such a loud response. Is it his size (he looks like he could ingest Nils Lofgren in one bite)? Is it his race (Robert Christgau once suggested that there were more people of color onstage during a Springsteen concert than in the arena audience)?

Let's hold on to that "race" question for a moment. Starting with *Born to Run*, Springsteen's music became more traditional, mainstream, white rock'n'roll. The jazz and R&B that colored the first two albums, especially the second, are missing in almost everything that follows. He still plays glorious R&B covers and makes occasional forays into contemporary R&B (as in the modified hip-hop beats of "Streets of Philadelphia" and "The Fuse"). A cynic could note that whitening his music made Springsteen more popular, but that would be too simple a charge, since roughly 99.9 percent of all rock'n'roll music is derived from African-American sources. But the fact is that Springsteen's subsequent records from '75 on are "whiter" than what came before. Although Springsteen would never have a part of it, he was often lauded by the rockist, racist antidisco movement of the late seventies: the great white hope and all that. That may not have been his intention, but it happened. Similarly, there's no way Springsteen woke up one morning and decided, "Hey, I should reduce Clemons's role in my music." It simply happened.

Perhaps Clemons serves a nostalgic function to the E Street audience, reminding them of what the band used to sound like way back when Springsteen used to lean on the Big Man on an album cover, back when they first learned of Springsteen and the band.

If so, of all the members of the E Street Band, Clemons is the one most stuck in a role, in the studio and onstage. In the studio, he's the one member of the band who has to hope that Springsteen writes a part for his instrument. The other members don't have to sit in the bullpen and wait for a call from the dugout. Onstage (to use the *Rising* tour, the most recent full tour as I write this, as an example), he's always there: playing percussion, singing backup, but most nights Clemons doesn't play much sax, and then it's often on a warhorse from *Born to Run* or *The River*, with a solo that is extremely close to the original recorded version. His '74 and '75 solos on "Spirit in the Night," for example, are more surprising than those since '78. He's playing a role, but it doesn't have to be this way. During the Vote for Change mini-tour, Clemons hurled thunderbolts through Bob Dylan's "All Along the Watchtower" (Neil Young guested, so of course they were covering the Hendrix version, a recasting so powerful even Dylan adopted it). Clemons still has it; the question is whether, except for a brief period ending in the early eighties, there's much room in Springsteen's music for what he offers. Too many times, both onstage and in his more recent work with the E Street Band, particularly *The Rising*, his solos feel like cameos, something grafted on top of a completed arrangement, rather than something organic coming out of it.

At least Clemons was all over *Born to Run*, inside and out (his image takes up a quarter of the back cover). It's less clear where Danny Federici was during the recording of that album. I recognize that the credits, as they are on so many Springsteen albums, are sketchy and sometimes wrong. (It's Suki Lahav on distinctive violin at the beginning of "Jungleland," but she receives no credit.) Sometimes session guys step in, like when Harold Davis slips an understated bass into "Meeting Across the River," but Gary Tallent does play bass on the album's other seven cuts. On *Born to Run*, Federici is credited only on the title track, cut at 914 Sound long before the Record Plant sessions that brought in the rest of the album. Bittan overdubbed organ after laying down piano tracks (piano came first, in large part because Springsteen wrote so many of the *Born to Run* songs on piano, rather than guitar). For whatever reason Federici wasn't there, his absence cuts a bit into the armor of the myth of the E Street Band.

The folks who do play on the record deliver a great diversity of music, from the rumbling barrage of barre chords that starts "Night" to the dramatic introduction of "Backstreets" that says as much about heartbreak as the lyrics that follow. The lyrics are all over the place, too. This is not a record in which Springsteen the wordsmith searches for tiny details like the "nursery mouth" of the first album's "For You." Some of the record is hilariously overblown, like the opening lines from "Jungleland": "The Rangers had a homecoming/In Harlem late last night." A hockey celebration in Harlem? Late at night? In the seventies? Are you nuts? But "Jungleland," like so many of the songs on *Born to Run*, is going for the mythic rather than the specific (and before you think that Springsteen used *Born to Run* to jettison the idea of extended songs, note that "Backstreets" tops six minutes and "Jungleland" clocks in at nearly 10). *Born to Run* is a record in which overall concept trumps individual songs. "Meeting Across the River" is a bit of ersatz *West Side Story* on its own, but presented as an overture to "Jungleland" it gains muscle. One early track listing opened with an acoustic "Thunder Road" and ended with the full-band take. It's all about the album.

When you listen to the outtakes from *Born to Run* that have shown up on *Tracks* and sundry unofficial sources, you can hear how Springsteen and his band and producers attacked songs in many different ways before they arrived at the right version. There are many attempts at "Born to Run," some with Suki Lahav's voice hovering in the background, some with more strings. "Thunder Road" is considered from all directions: sax in the beginning instead of harmonica, guitar at the end instead of sax. "Night" and others are attempted with double-tracked vocals (bad idea). The most intriguing alternate take that has surfaced, at least in collector circles, is one of "Backstreets" featuring Gamble-and-Huff-derived strings, a stunning mix of rock'n'roll production values with the Philly Soul of the moment. Of the other leftovers, "A Love So Fine," a rewrite of the Chiffons hit of the same name, is light, fun, and of a piece with the party music on *The Wild, the Innocent, and the E Street Shuffle*, this time with more compact drumming. "So Young and in Love" from *Tracks* is essentially "A Love So Fine" with a different chorus. Whatever the title, the song offers up a delicious sax solo and it sounds like one of those songs from the second album, perhaps because it was probably recorded at 914. "Linda Let Me Be the One," released on *Tracks*, is a look forward toward the ballad style of *The River*, particularly "I Wanna Marry You." "Lovers in the Cold" is an uncompleted song that donated some music to "Thunder Road."

Let's not leave *Born to Run* before listening to "Thunder Road" one more time. The song, despite the couplet "Tonight we'll be free/All the promises will be broken" is about a promise yet to be kept (indeed, Springsteen would record a follow-on to "Thunder Road" called "The Promise," in which everything is broken and it's no fun). It's a young man about to break free, albeit tentatively. Listening to the studio takes of "Thunder Road," it's difficult to believe that by the *Rising* tour, the song would be reduced to something downtempo, a dirge even when played with the band. Springsteen and the E Street Band are 30 years older than they were when they first recorded the song. They're richer, wiser, less wide-eyed. Some of Springsteen's songs respond well to being reconceptualized (there's a downer solo-acoustic version of "The Promised Land" that works). "Thunder Road" isn't one of them. They got it right with the initial release.

Plenty of people must have felt they got the record right, because *Born to Run* made Springsteen a genuine rock star. With the record done at last, the band hit the road, most famously in a hot radio broadcast at Manhattan's Bottom Line. The songs and the band had developed since the Main Point broadcast. They had changed, sharpened their attack, gotten less weird. *Born to Run* may not have been a better record than *The Wild, the Innocent, and the E Street Shuffle,* but it was certainly a better mainstream rock'n'roll record. It landed Springsteen on the covers of *Time* and *Newsweek* simultaneously, it guaranteed his songs the attention they deserved, and it led to the breakdown of his relationship with manager and producer Mike Appel. In retrospect, the split was a long time coming, but it was exacerbated and made inevitable by the arrival of Jon Landau. The disagreement between Springsteen and Appel ended up in court and kept Springsteen on the road to make a living and out of a recording studio until June '77, when, with Landau and Springsteen producing, the E Street Band began the lengthy sessions that yielded *Darkness on the Edge of Town* in June '78.

There are two published versions of the Spring-steen/Appel breakup, both of which have axes to grind. In Dave Marsh's selective *Born to Run*, the first of his Springsteen books (they're updated and repackaged occasionally; the latest version is *Two Hearts*, a 696-page attempt to get it all between two covers) makes Appel out as the sole heavy and doesn't much address the legal record. That record, sealed, appeared as part of *Down Thunder Road: The Making of Bruce Spring-steen*, credited to "Marc Eliot with the participation of Mike Appel." Eliot's book is terrible, full of overheated writing and the sort of look-at-me stories that deposed managers tell, like how they prevented the star from being attacked physically by evil club owners and their proxies. As a piece of literature, its value falls some-where between that of a year-old newspaper Help Wanted section and a high school term paper on why Kansas's "Dust in the Wind" is really profound. But it does offer something rather marvelous that makes it worth taking out from the library or shoplifting: It includes many of the depositions and court documents associated with the lawsuits. If you ever wanted to read transcriptions of Springsteen shouting and cursing in front of lawyers, it's the book for you. The transcripts are entertaining and embarrassing, but there is a truth behind them: Springsteen felt his career was out of his control and he wanted it back. He got it.

You'd never know it by reading *Down Thunder Road*, which I promise never to mention again after this quote: "*Darkness on the Edge of Town* is today considered by all parties involved to be an artistic failure, the worst of Springsteen's albums. Bruce has often spoken of his wish to somehow be able to redo it." (Needless to say, Eliot's selective "Sources and Notes" at the end of the book offer no actual evidence for any of those assertions.) Almost the exact opposite is true. *Darkness on the Edge of Town* has its flaws, but it was the album on which Springsteen found the topic—decency in the face of defeat—that would fuel a quarter century of writing. Four of its 10 songs—"Badlands," "The Promised Land," "Prove It All Night," and the title number—remain among the core songs he performs almost every night, with or without the E Street Band.

It was not a quick album to make. Work at one high-priced studio proved fruitless, so the band packed up and returned to the Record Plant . . . for a long time. In *Backstreets*, the compilation book put out by Charles R. Cross and his staff at the magazine of the same name (under new management, it's still wonderful, even the statistical minutiae that would impress even diehard sabermetricians: 1818 Airport Road #300, Chapel Hill NC 27514), we learn that the version of "Prove It All Night" on the record was take 49, "Racing in the Street" was take 46, and so on. They worked these songs long and hard. The sessions to *Darkness on the Edge of Town*, *The River*, and *Born in the U.S.A.* have been widely bootlegged and those illicit recordings reveal someone who would not let go of a good song until he had considered it from as many directions as he could imagine. The music of one song would be spliced into the lyrics of another, solos would appear and disappear, tempos would vary wildly. After the split from his original manager and producer and with the heightened expectations that come from this being the first record he cut knowing there was an audience for it, Springsteen wanted to make a distinct, personal statement.

The first part of that statement was sonic. *Darkness on the Edge of Town* had a much different sound from *Born to Run*. The Wall of Sound method of its predecessor was replaced by something more stripped down, echoey, airier, with more distance between the instruments. The biggest difference was in the sound of the drums. Remember, this was the late seventies, long before anything could easily be sampled or synthesized. Like pitchers and catchers reporting to spring training early, drummers and engineers would arrive at a recording studio a week or two early to get an acceptable drum sound when the other position players arrived. Graham Parker, who later worked with Jimmy Iovine (engineer of *Darkness*), once told me "this was the age of the Quest for the Perfect Drum Sound." The sound of *Darkness* was more about clarity than power. The idea, I suppose, was that clarity would yield power. More guitar, too: After the piano-based *Born to Run*, clenched songs like "Adam Raised a Cain," "Candy's Room," and "Streets of Fire" deliver the most guitar on a Springsteen LP since "Kitty's Back."

The stories on this record were less majestic than those on *Born to Run*. For one thing, no one is escaping anything. The father and son in "Adam Raised a Cain" are stuck in eternal conflict, those trying to flee in "Something in the Night" don't make it out of state, the men in "Factory" walk to work "with death in their eyes," and the narrator in "Streets of Fire" is so dislocated he talks "to only strangers." By returning to his telephoto lens, Springsteen kept the songs stretched tight: Eight of the ten songs (the most-ever on a Springsteen album thus far) clocked in at under five minutes, and you'd be hard-pressed to find much fat on any of them. The three songs meant to be rousing anthems— "Badlands," "The Promised Land," and "Prove It All Night"—are modest in their dreams. In "Badlands," the most the singer can think to ask for is "one face that ain't looking through me." The word *believe* shows up in both "Badlands" and "The Promised Land": The singer believes despite little evidence to justify it.

The two finest songs on *Darkness on the Edge of Town*, the ballads that close either side of the album, are about belief, too. "Racing in the Street" is not a happy tale: auto racer picks up girl, settles down with girl, can't connect to girl, races cars to keep himself sane. In its final verse, he talks about what he wants to believe in, but the performance suggests that the singer knows there's little reason for his belief. The narrator has spent an entire song documenting his estrangement. But he wants to rescue himself and his girl and his colleagues, and the band makes it sound like he can. Organist Federici, again an emphatic member of the E Street Band (he contributes a sharp break to "Prove It All Night"), and pianist Bittan lock in together, leading the band through a gorgeous coda that reminds you how moving rock-'n'roll can be when words don't get in the way. They deliver the peace the narrator can only hope for.

The album's title track finds a similar character; perhaps it's meant to be the same guy some time later, after instead of riding to the sea with the narrator the woman has left him, living well "in a style she's trying to maintain." He's still racing. He can't stop. Only alone can he get past the "things [that] don't seem to matter much to me now." "Darkness on the Edge of Town" is a slow, snarling, burning rocker, coiled so tightly you're afraid what might happen if the singer were to cut loose. He doesn't. The narrator is stuck on the top of some hill somewhere, but Springsteen the writer isn't, because that's where he has found, as he put it, "my adult voice."

That's writer's voice, not singer's voice. As on *Born to Run*, here Springsteen sings in an exaggerated low voice that makes many of the songs sound more subdued than they'd be otherwise. That ended once he left the studio. When the band performed onstage, the songs couldn't have been more alive.

In the studio, Springsteen and the E Street Band left behind many lighter numbers, some of them quite good, that soared live but didn't fit in with the prickly tone of *Darkness on the Edge of Town*. Most of the best of them came out on *Tracks*. "Rendezvous" was too light for any record, "Iceman" was too boring, and "Hearts of Stone" was a soul ballad that earned a "Send to Southside Johnny" stamp. But the loose, sparkling "Give the Girl a Kiss" should at least have been released as a B-side, so its bar-band liveliness could temper the darkness on the other side of the seven-inch. (With *The River*, Springsteen would start releasing non-LP B-sides.) "Don't Look Back," a straight-ahead rocker, made it onto early track listings but wound up being recorded by The Knack, who released their version long before *Tracks* arrived.

What you hear in these songs is a world broader than that depicted on *Darkness on the Edge of Town*, a world in which people smiled and even danced every now and then. It would be explored on the double album *The River* ('80), a varied collection that grew out of the long tour behind *Darkness*. That tour was a huge success for the E Street Band, both commercially (they moved up from theaters to arenas in many markets) and artistically. Almost every night, some wonderful cover would slip into the set. Usually it was a medley of songs associated with Mitch Ryder and the Detroit Wheels; other nights it could be "You Can't Sit Down," "Quarter to Three," "I Fought the Law," "Heartbreak Hotel," "Raise Your Hand," "Oh Boy," or many more. Unreleased songs were aired regularly, too, among them the summer instrumental "Paradise

110

by the C," "Because the Night" (a hit for Patti Smith), "Fire" (a hit for the Pointer Sisters, not a hit for Robert Gordon), "The Fever," and "The Promise," a sad new ballad, the tense flip-side sequel to "Thunder Road." (The first three songs can be found on the *Live 1975/85* box; the final pair justify the existence of *18 Tracks*.) As the tour went on, more and more songs that would eventually find their way onto *The River* leaked into the set.

The heart of the show was the new *Darkness* material; most nights the band would play seven or eight of those songs. "Racing in the Street" earned a crowning coda, and Springsteen's loud, nasty guitar was everywhere, particularly an elongated (more than 10 minutes some nights) "Prove It All Night," which built from a soft piano intro through a screaming guitar solo into an unruly version of the song as it appeared on the album, followed by another wicked guitar solo. It was as if Springsteen intended in one song to make up for all the guitar solos he didn't play onstage in '75 and '76.

Every night, the second set would end with "Rosalita (Come Out Tonight)." In the middle of the song, Springsteen would often call for a breakdown, during which he'd introduce the band members. Sometimes it was perfunctory, often it was funny. The breakdown would end with Springsteen and Clemons at opposite ends of the stage, slowly walking toward one another until they met at the center-stage microphone, yelled, "Turn it up" into that microphone, and turned away

111

from one another to continue the song. But before they turned away, many nights they'd do one other thing together. They'd kiss.

They'd kiss? Indeed, Springsteen has kissed Clemons onstage far more than he has his own wife, who's been in the band for many hundreds of shows. If a Bruce-Clarence kiss happened once, it would provide an amusing anecdote, but for a time it became almost as regular a part of the set as "Rosalita" itself. I suspect they did it to be funny and a bit provocative. Provocative to whom? Let's sketch the worst caricature of a rock'n'roll fan: drunk, stupid, racist, homophobic. These are not straw men I'm conjuring up. Go to any arena or stadium show and you'll find them. There was a time, not so far in the past, when Springsteen's image would cater to that crowd: Think of the overbuilt guy who fronted the band on the *Born in the U.S.A.* stadium tour, all oversize gestures, decked out in bandana, muscle t-shirt, and work boots. These were not people whose attraction to Springsteen was based on his ability to write songs that worked for the Pointer Sisters and Donna Summer. It's possible that, long before Springsteen became an action figure, the "Rosalita" kiss was a kiss-off to that crew. And before you read anything more into the act, remember this is just a rock'n'roll show. What do people say they do onstage at a rock-'n'roll show? They don't say they work—they play. When they pucker up, Springsteen and Clemons are playing with race and sex, in one act playing with all sorts of white-rock sexual taboos. Not everyone saw the fun in it. Semioticians in the audience may have read Martha Nell Smith's unsubtle academic essay, "Sexual Mobilities in Bruce Springsteen: Performance as Quality," in which she thinks long and hard about all that kissing, and concludes of Springsteen that "Homoeroticism permeates his performances, assumption of the female is one of his repeated artistic maneuvers, and even though he writes and sings about Adam, he finally seems more like Eve in his approach to knowledge." In case you were wondering.

While recording their next album at the Power Station studio in New York in '79, the band took a break to play two nights at Madison Square Garden headlining the MUSE concerts. MUSE stood for Musicians United for Safe Energy and the "No Nukes" concerts were intended to raise money for antinuclear causes. Several months earlier, while starting the sessions for what was then thought to be a single album, tentatively titled *The Ties That Bind*, Springsteen and the band had recorded "Roulette," a tale of justified paranoia written in the shadow of the near-catastrophe at Three Mile Island. Although that song didn't make the resulting album (it emerged as a *Tunnel of Love* B-side in '88) or the MUSE set list, apparently Springsteen's distrust of the nuclear power industry was enough to prod him to make his first public political statement since he'd played a George McGovern benefit in '72. (Alas, the MUSE concerts were just as effective in stopping nuclear power as the McGovern benefit was in unseating Nixon.) The shows were quite good, stripped-down versions of the *Darkness* set, with a new ballad, "The River," added, as well as a cover of Maurice Williams and the Zodiacs' "Stay," on which Jackson Browne joined. (For an amusing personal account of the MUSE performance, see Eric Alterman's *It Ain't No Sin to Be Glad You're Alive: The Promise of Bruce Springsteen.* The book offers the occasional labored insight, but it's perfect if what you really want to know is whether Alterman's attendance at the MUSE concert prevented him from attending Kol Nidre services.)

Alterman was one of many people choosing their idol those nights in September '79, and the extra-large reaction that Springsteen received led him to rethink the album he thought he had completed. It also caused him to rethink his set. In an interview a year later, Steve Van Zandt spoke warmly of the compact MUSE shows and said they felt sufficient to him, but then noted that Springsteen merely added the length of those shows to the long set they were playing already. Even in print, you can hear how exhausted Van Zandt sounds. But for now, the band was a long way away from hitting the stage again. The rejected album, as indicated by a Power Station tape box, included 10 songs:

Side One
The Ties That Bind
Cindy

Hungry Heart
Stolen Car
Be True

Side Two
The River
You Can Look (But You Better Not Touch)
The Price You Pay
I Wanna Marry You
Loose Ends

Seven of those songs ended up on the final version of *The River*, in some cases in wildly different versions, and two of the remaining three have been released subsequently. Why wasn't this record good enough to come out? *The Ties That Bind* would have been a lighter record than *Darkness on the Edge of Town*: only "Stolen Car," "The River," and "Loose Ends" carried the bleak intensity of the previous album. "The Ties That Bind" was an optimistic rocker; "Cindy" and "Hungry Heart" turned failed relationships into jokes or near-jokes, "You Can Look" was giddy rockabilly, and both "The Price You Pay" and "I Wanna Marry You" are, to varying degrees, pure romantic ballads. "The Price You Pay" slips a bit of iconoclasm into the "Promised Land" formula; "I Wanna Marry You" is a straight soul ballad, drenched in tremolo guitar.

What was missing was, of all things, a sense of extremes. Consider the songs Springsteen added when the record blossomed into the two-LP *The River*, and

115

you'll note that nearly all of them capture emotional outliers. "Out in the Street," "Crush on You," and "Ramrod" may be the happiest and least introspective songs in his catalogue; "Point Blank" and "Fade Away" are certainly among his most pessimistic and helpless depictions of life and love gone wrong. Working with 20 songs, Springsteen and the E Street Band could cover more ground without feeling that one wrong sequencing decision could tip the record too far in one direction or the other. With *The River* (released on October 17, '80, the same day as another landmark, expansive album by an American band, Talking Heads' *Remain in Light*), Springsteen started making records as broad, loose, diverse, and entertaining as his concerts—and as dramatic as those concerts. There's plenty of grit and evil here—I count several accidental deaths and at least one narrator-performed murder—but there are also a handful of some of the happiest and most liberating performances of his career. With this double album, all the voices arguing in Springsteen's head could go public at last. And it all came out of one head. The sly frat-rocker "Sherry Darling" could be what one of his characters was projecting publicly; "Fade Away" or "Wreck on the Highway" could depict what the same guy was feeling inside.

The River is the one studio album by Bruce Springsteen and the E Street Band that sounds the most like their live shows, which may be why it stands as one of their most enduring. Springsteen's singing in the studio is natural again. The reason might be the one member of the E Street Band whose playing is least relevant to the sound of Springsteen's records but whose contribution to the final product, in this case, is inestimable. Steve Van Zandt's guitar was never that important to the sound of Springsteen's records, but his production aesthetic (he produced the record along with Springsteen and Landau) helps make *The River* unique. The album has the intensity of *Darkness on the Edge of Town* but also, on songs like the effortless-sounding party "Sherry Darling," allows more verve than any Springsteen record since *The Wild, the Innocent, and the E Street Shuffle*. Perhaps the best example of what Van Zandt's influence brought to the production is "The Ties That Bind," the first song on the record. Van Zandt's productions for Southside Johnny and the Asbury Jukes (and, later, Gary U.S. Bonds and others) were about playing close to the heart, never relying on tricks, and emphasizing the unit over individual players, even when guiding a group as technically astute as the Jukes' horn section. Drop the needle on *The River*: Out of the darkness, a snare shot announces the record and the band dives in, coalescing and separating, supporting the vocal or pushing it forward, depending on what's necessary. Along with "Ramrod," it's Max Weinberg's most propulsive performance on the double album: He squeezes in as much as he can, making every turnaround count, without one beat too many. Listen to his unprecedented work under the sunny sax solo,

117

especially the double snare shot midway that demands everyone push higher and harder. At the end of that solo, you can hear five glorious chords in quick succession, the rest of the E Street Band reaching Weinberg's level: hands full but not too busy. Weinberg maintains that level throughout the double album, coupling fluently with Gary Tallent's bass. The bass serves double duty on the record, providing both melody and foundation, the link between drums and the rest of the band. Weinberg had pulled this off once before with Van Zandt, stepping in to fill a drum vacancy during the recording of the Jukes's top album, *Hearts of Stone*. While only a handful of songs on the released *River* would approximate soul music (three ballads: "I Wanna Marry You," "Fade Away," and especially "Drive All Night"), it's Van Zandt's approach to soul music—direct communication, play what you feel, let everyone see it—that defined the emotional extremes of the record and tied them together. And perhaps because he was more connected to (or felt more responsible for) the overall sound of the album, Van Zandt's harmonies on the live-sounding "Jackson Cage," "Two Hearts," and "Point Blank" and many others, make far more of a vocal impact on *The River* than any of the previous Springsteen records with which he was involved. It was about time and it was just in time: This would be his last time in the studio with the E Street Band for a full record for a long time. After the '80–'81 tour he left the band for a solo career, though he was back in place at various times since, including sundry reunion activities.

That soulfulness was dictated by Springsteen's songs, more mature and cutting more deeply. "Independence Day" continued the intergenerational warfare of *Darkness on the Edge of Town*'s "Adam Raised a Cain" (and Springsteen's overdramatic extension of the Animals' "It's My Life," which he played live on occasion), now with more chance of accommodation and a sense that things are out of their control.

The mood is much different on the next song, "Hungry Heart," a spacious Phil Spector exercise, or an example of what Spector records might have sounded like if Hal Blaine was unavailable and Phil called in Al Jackson to cover. Even happier is "Out in the Street," a weekend song in the mold of the Easybeats' "Friday on My Mind." When Springsteen and Van Zandt trade vocals at the end, the sense of community is almost palpable, something that expanded live when other band members (first Clemons, in later tours Nils Lofgren and Patti Scialfa) took their turns. It was a myth, of course: No matter how welcome and reliable the paychecks were, there's no way all these people were this happy with each other all the time. You go on the road with six other people for a year, even in sometimes luxurious circumstances, and everything about them you dislike will make itself apparent to you every day. Van Zandt mugs around the stage like a cross between a wiggy Dean Martin, Keith Richards, and Patchy the Pirate from *Spongebob Squarepants*: Imagine living on a bus with that. But "Out in the Street," which the band played nearly every night for several tours, shows the E Street Band as the audience wants them to be, perhaps as the band members themselves want to be and sometimes are.

Carrying less baggage, "Crush on You" is joyously dumb with its references to Venus de Milo and Sheena of the Jungle, both identified as inferior to the object of the singer's crush. (Similarly, "Cadillac Ranch" namechecks Burt Reynolds and "I'm a Rocker" cites Columbo, Kojak, and *Mission Impossible*, not exactly paragons of high culture.) The band smashes into the last verse of "Crush on You" like a bar band told by a club owner that if they play just a little harder they'll actually get the $50 he promised each of them.

The first disc of *The River* climaxes with the title track, which debuted at the MUSE Concerts and signaled the beginning of something new in Springsteen's writing. He still wanted his songs to speak for everyman, as many of them did on *Born to Run* and *Darkness on the Edge of Town*, but now he did so by giving his characters and settings a new level of precise, writerly detail—pulling his lover close just to feel her breathe—that made the song concrete, not just a tale of imagined everypeople. Other ballads followed the same method. In "Fade Away," the beauty of the arrangement can't hide the pain lurking behind. The singer worries he might become "just some other ghost out on

120

the street to whom you stop and politely speak when you pass on by," and in the next song, "Stolen Car" he does turn into a ghost. Quiet, distant, the song is the sound of a hollowed-out man, driving in circles, lost forever from the woman he loves, hoping he gets caught in his stolen car so he is forced to connect with another human being, but he can't even make that happen: "Each night I wait to get caught/But I never do." A very different version of the song was intended for the unreleased '79 album. It's a grander performance, featuring the whole band, with a Cinemascope feel, and it takes the song deeper. The singer dreams he's allowed to come home, reenacts his wedding, and as he leans to kiss his bride, it all evaporates.

If you think that's as lonely as a Springsteen narrator can get, you ain't heard nothing yet. There's a dream at the center of "Point Blank," which had been played in early versions on the *Darkness* tour. Opening the second half of *The River*, it gets even darker. It was tried many ways in the studio, sometimes with a fierce guitar solo, but the released version features a snarling, repetitive organ circling around the tale of promises blasted to smithereens. The narrator tells the story of a former lover condemned to a life in the shadows, and his emotions range from regretful to contemplative to murderous. It's unclear whether the woman in question is living off a welfare check or living off turning tricks, but it is clear that she's gone from the narrator forever. The singer dreams of seeing her "back home in those old clubs/the way we used to be" (a less psychotic version of that dream appears in the *Born in the U.S.A.* outtake "None But the Brave," available on the *Essential* bonus disc) and then confronts her or someone he thinks is her "last night down on the avenue" and shoots her (or the person he thinks is her) dead. Their emotional deaths end in her physical death, which has resolved nothing: He's still addressing the song to her corpse.

The album moves from "Point Blank" into the festive "Cadillac Ranch." The beat and guitar riff of "Cadillac Ranch" provide an instant release of tension after the heaviness of "Point Blank." The two-second space between those two songs traces the wide distance Springsteen and the E Street Band cover on *The River*. But as strong as the released album is, it's far from the whole story. Along with *Born in the U.S.A.*, *The River* offers roughly an album's worth of release-worthy outtakes. *The River*, indeed, would have been a much more consistent triple album than *Sandinista!*, the big, fat, in-your-face triple LP the Clash released two months after Springsteen's record release, in part as a taunting response. At least a dozen of the rockers—"Restless Nights," "Roulette," "Dollhouse," "Where the Bands Are," "Loose Ends," "Living on the Edge of the World," "Take 'Em as They Come," "Be True," "Ricky Wants a Man of Her Own," "I Wanna Be With You," "From Small Things (Big Things One Day Come)," "Held Up Without a Gun"—are as strong as the songs that were released on the album, and they all have been released subsequently. When many of them were included on *Tracks*, Van Zandt ruefully cited these songs as among his favorites, "each one a lost argument." A triple album would have been a bit much, but there were enough top-flight songs to fill one.

The songs were there onstage, too, more than 30 of them most nights. During the tour behind *The River*, the E Street Band's legendary three-hour shows gradually expanded into legendary four-hour shows. Alternately ferocious and silly, peaking at Nassau, these shows unified the disparate strands of rock'n'roll, everything from all-out punk to Christmas music, from "Point Blank" to "Cadillac Ranch." These were the band's loosest shows in years, full of surprises like covers appropriate to location and calendar: "On Top of Old Smokey" in Portland, near Mt. St. Helens; "Waltz Across Texas" in Austin; "Haunted House" in Los Angeles on Halloween night, with Bruce emerging from a coffin; the warhorse "Santa Claus Is Coming to Town," and "Merry Christmas Baby" to personalize the Nassau shows. Different cities saw similar sets under different circumstances. An intense show in Philadelphia the night after John Lennon was murdered began with Springsteen explaining from the stage why he felt he had to play that night even if he didn't want to and ended with a "Twist and Shout" that rocked all the way to heaven. The tour also hinted toward his political awakening. At a show in Tempe the night after the Reagan landslide, he said, "I don't know what you guys think about what happened last night, but I think it's pretty frightening." By the time the band reached Uniondale, Springsteen was offering onstage book reports of Allan Nevins and Henry Steele Commanger's *Pocket History of the United States* and Joe Klein's *Woody Guthrie: A Life*, following the latter with a mournful "This Land Is Your Land."

This search took time. By New Year's Eve in Nassau, the length of the show had turned extreme: 38 songs, more than four hours, more than one-third longer than the show that had opened the tour three months earlier in Ann Arbor, Michigan, where Springsteen began his quest by forgetting the words to "Born to Run." He was looking for something and he would not relinquish the stage until he found it. He led the best band in the land but he wanted something new. Something extreme.

Chapter 4

The Jersey Devil

North of Jamaica, Jimmy Cliff was never much of a hitmaker. He was best known to American eyes and ears from his performance as Ivan, the unrepentant star of the seventies Jamaican rude boy film *The Harder They Come*, and, more important, as the singer of several songs on the movie's soundtrack, especially "You Can Get It If You Really Want," "Many Rivers to Cross," and the title track. His appearances on the U.S. *Billboard* charts tended to be brief and unimpressive and there hasn't been one since '93. Cliff's importance in Jamaica shouldn't be understated—he has an Order of Merit to his name—but all but the most obsessive reggae fans in the United States know him most for his string of late sixties and early seventies masterpieces, those from *The Harder They Come* as well as "Viet Nam" and "Wonderful World, Beautiful People." He doesn't record much anymore, but all of his records are worth hearing—except for the ones in which he tries a little too hard to cross over to pop music.

What's most interesting about Cliff being a reggae icon is that he isn't a reggae singer. From the start, even under the tutelage of Leslie Kong, a producer whose reach and ambition was so wide that Greil Marcus likened him to a Jamaican Sam Phillips (*The "King" King Collection*, which came out on Mango in '81, is a superb introduction, although it includes no Cliff cuts), Cliff adopted the vernacular of American soul singers like Otis Redding and Sam Moore. Those are the performers he aspired to match. It made him distinct among his Jamaican competitors, but it didn't help him much in the Lower 48, where there was already one soul-singing reggae star, Toots Hibbert. (To be fair, Bob Marley started out wanting to be a soul singer, too, but his talents and ambitions turned out to be far broader.)

So, under the radar, Cliff kept recording, maintaining his base in Jamaica (and in countries with a strong Jamaican connection like England), but not being confused with someone who sold lots of records. Pick up any of the many anthologies of Cliff's seventies work post–*The Harder They Come*, and you'll hear someone whose lack of superstardom hasn't prevented him from recording a series of lively reggae-soul songs that would have excited anyone who got a chance to listen, songs like "Trapped," in which funky rhythm guitar and carnival organ give way to deliberate vocals and corkscrew horns, all pushing forward the story of someone in terrible circumstances who is convinced he'll persevere . . . someday.

That particular song eventually got the attention it deserved, thanks to an unlikely conveyor. Except for a brief (four shows in a week), unhappy (the artist whose face was on them is alleged to have torn down the hype-driving banners for his show in London) trip at the height of *Born to Run* mania, Bruce Springsteen and the E Street Band had never performed in Europe until a two-month, 34-date stint in the spring of '81. A London date right before the end of that much more successful foray featured "Trapped," which Springsteen had first heard on a Cliff cassette he bought at an Amsterdam airport a month earlier. That's right: A random purchase in a departure lounge can alter a superstar's set list.

The band altered "Trapped" profoundly. (Aside from live versions in '88 of "Get Up, Stand Up" and "Part Man, Part Monkey," the E Street Band didn't do reggae. About as close as Springsteen got was sharing a bill early in his career at Max's Kansas City with Bob Marley.) They replaced rhythm guitar with chicken-scratch guitar and ethereal synthesizer, with most of the feeling of triumph excised. The new music for the song uses tense verses and offers some release in the rocking choruses and Clemons's tough solo, but this isn't standard rock'n'roll tension-and-release. When Springsteen sings lines like "I know someday I'll walk out of here," it seems more like a hope than a promise. The band

127

never recorded this song in the studio, although a live version cut in '84 appears on the *We Are the World* self-lovefest and (pick this one instead) the bonus disc of *Essential*, where the performance is credited to the '81 band despite Patti Scialfa and Nils Lofgren being clearly audible among the singers.

"Trapped" was one of three semicovers the band debuted on the Europe '81 tour, performances that hinted where Springsteen was going as he began to think about his next record. "Follow That Dream" was a version of the title track of a B-minus Elvis Presley vehicle from '62 (The King plays a guitar player from New Jersey's Pine Barrens named Toby Kwimper and that's all you need to know about the film) that bore little relation to the slick version on the big screen. Slowed down from the movie version, lyrics like "When I find her I may find out/Just what my dreams are all about" are a bit vague but still something you might imagine Springsteen himself writing.

Unlike the light-hearted original, the band plays the song slow, serious, sometimes borderline-mournful. Without changing many of the words, they gave the song a new, deeper tone.

The third new entry to the set, "Johnny Bye Bye," was an exhaustive overhaul of Chuck Berry's "Bye Bye Johnny." It starts with Berry's timeless opening couplet "She drew out all her money from a Southern Trust/And put her little boy aboard a Greyhound bus," but unlike the Berry original, in which the mother taking the bank withdrawal is sending her son out to an unequivocally happy life, this rewrite eventually turns the sad light of truth back on Elvis.

When Springsteen recorded the song (it didn't make *Born in the U.S.A.*), he changed "nothing" to "trouble," which feels a bit vaguer. Little else about either the Berry or Springsteen versions of the take is vague. In Berry's original (which Springsteen has played live on occasion, at least once with Joe Grushecky and the Iron City Houserockers), "Bye Bye Johnny" is a sequel to "Johnny B. Goode," the story of what happens when the guitar-slinger comes back to his hometown accompanied by his Hollywood bride. It's all happy ending. In Springsteen's hands, it becomes a story about wasted opportunity. Taken along with the downer "Trapped" and the quiet but more hopeful "Follow That Dream," these new performances add up to the work of someone, now a star himself, looking around and trying to make sure he can still think clearly, despite all the money and fame threatening to cloud his vision. With one song called "Trapped" and two songs either associated with or about a legendary performer who felt trapped, you could hear Springsteen promising himself which path he would never go down.

Back in the United States for the summer of '81, the tour ran for two more months, all extended residences in the band's top markets (New Jersey, Philadelphia, Cleveland, Washington, Detroit, Denver, Los Angeles, San Diego, Chicago, and Cincinnati). Some nights were disconcerting (a firecracker dropped onto the stage from the upper deck one night at the Brendan Byrne Spaceship in East Rutherford), others were full of welcome guest stars (Southside Johnny some nights, Gary U.S. Bonds—whose E Street-fueled comeback was at its peak—and others), and one in particular was remarkably intense. On August 20, the band played a benefit in Los Angeles for the Vietnam Veterans of America. It was a night of heightened emotion and political statements. Springsteen talked more than usual that night, not to tell the usual light stories, but to talk about what Americans owed the people sent to fight a pointless war, why it could happen again if Americans weren't vigilant, and how the history of this country was full of times when "you end up a victim and how you don't even know it." It all poured out of him that night, directly, intimately: Springsteen's slow education in what happened to the veterans, his growing respect for them, his anger at how they were treated, and—even though he never said it explicitly—his mixed feelings over having missed the war himself (he flunked his induction physical). During "The River," a song that hit close to Springsteen's own life—the song is about his sister's experiences—he was so full of emotion he missed several lines of the lyric and had to regain his composure as the band gently carried him.

That concert for the veterans changed Springsteen and his music. Concert-goers noted that immediately. In the shows between that Los Angeles date and the end of

130

the tour three weeks later, audiences would hear Springsteen turn to covers, as if he had yet to write the new stories he now wanted to tell. It was in the voices of his heroes he would speak now, offering up plenty of John Fogerty ("Who'll Stop the Rain," "Run Through the Jungle," "Rockin' All Over the World," and "Proud Mary") and Woody Guthrie ("This Land Is Your Land" and "Deportee [Plane Wreck at Los Gatos]"). The tour ended in Cincinnati on September 14. It would be nearly three years before the E Street Band played again onstage as a unit and by then Van Zandt would be long out of the group, having become "Little Steven" and embarked on his fascinating, borderline-quixotic solo career. After Cincinnati, Springsteen went home, read, watched movies, and wrote fast. Right after New Year's Day in '82, he sat down at his home in Colts Neck, New Jersey, with his guitar tech Mike Batlan and a four-track Teac cassette recorder to cut demos for his next record with the E Street Band. Instead of writing songs in the studio, a technique that was partly to blame for how long it took to record both *Darkness on the Edge of Town* and *The River*, Springsteen intended to get his best new compositions on tape, present them to the band, and knock them out quickly in the studio.

In the first days of January '82, two Bruce Springsteens emerged. On January 3, one sat on a chair in his bedroom and cut the songs that would comprise his next record, the solo *Nebraska*, as tough-minded, scary, raw, and despairing a set of songs as he'd ever record.

On January 5, the other guy was onstage at the Stone Pony, playing ragged versions of "Jole Blon" and "In the Midnight Hour" with the locals in the Lord Gunner Group. It would be five years before Springsteen recorded a song with the chorus "Two faces have I," but he was living that way already.

Of course, the Two Bruces were each part of the same complicated man, and they lived out Springsteen's two outlier urges: the Artist, who only has to please himself, and the Performer, who's happiest after midnight at some hot, smoky, smelly club, playing Chuck Berry and Little Richard standards to appreciative, excited, tired, drunk, packed houses. He played so many of these clubs in the summer and fall of '82 that *Backstreets* would refer to those shows as the "1982 Tour of New Jersey." But aside from playing *Nebraska*'s "Open All Night" once, there was no overlap between what Springsteen had achieved with his Teac four-track and what he was doing on those club stages night after night.

Or was there? Perhaps the stories are interlocking. Consider the post-*River*, pre–*Born in the U.S.A.* Bruce, a man at the cusp of a tremendous artistic risk, followed by even more tremendous commercial success. *Nebraska* was a strange advance; those endless adventures on the Jersey shore bar circuit, where he'd play with pretty much any band that would take him as a relief from his real career as an arena rocker, were a retreat. But both his relentless clubbing and his dark acoustic record were products of the same impulse: to get deeper into the music.

It's not often mentioned how eccentric *Nebraska* is. It's true that when Springsteen sat on that rocking chair, he was not intending to record an album, just to get some songs down on tape to teach the band. But he was also thinking of these compositions as arranged performances, not just quickie demos. The Teac was a primitive machine, but it was still a four-track recorder that allowed for overdubbing. After he got down the basic take, Springsteen would add another guitar, a harmonica, a harmony, some percussion, even a synthesizer, to flesh out the sound. And then, instead of finishing there, he would mix what he had through an echoplex, adding more effects. He may not have been thinking in terms of a *finished* record, but he was thinking in terms of *making* a record. A strange record, a weird record, a collection of songs that would not bend when asked to adapt to the usual E Street treatment. As Springsteen put it in *Songs*, "I went into the studio, brought in the band, recorded, remixed, and succeeded in making the whole thing worse."

Nebraska keeps calling back listeners, with its specificity of musical, lyrical, and emotional detail, its remarkable pessimism, and its refusal to romanticize that pessimism. The last number on this solo acoustic album is "Reason to Believe," an illustration of why belief is sometimes the most bewildering joke of all. Fans and critics went into contortions trying to explain why that fatalistic tune was in fact some sort of affirmation (Springsteen's earlier work encouraged them to make such judgments). It wasn't.

Nebraska builds on the quiet that had entered Springsteen's music, both in songs like "The River" and "Wreck on the Highway" from the last record and in the three recent live debuts ("Trapped" had a fast part, but its quiet parts were very quiet for something intended to fill sports arenas). How quiet can you be and still make great emotional noise? I love *Nebraska* for its unconventionality, its dark humor, its obsessiveness, and its refusal to succumb to any rock'n'roll conventions despite being recorded by a very conventional rocker. *Nebraska* is a once-in-a-lifetime album, as close as Springsteen will ever get to blues feeling, if not blues form. (Steel Mill was enough on that front, thank you.) Many of these songs take place on some unknown highway at some ungodly hour, a lonely narrator begging for some connection to something, be it a woman, a job, a radio disc jockey, or a half-forgotten family. *Nebraska*, as much as Van Morrison's scarifying *Astral Weeks* or some late-night Takoma deliberation from John Fahey, is about being alone, about being desperate, about being brave enough to admit that there's no easy cure for desperation. It's an idea Springsteen would return to in "Dancing in the Dark" and for most of *Tunnel of Love*, but it's on *Nebraska* that rock'n'roll's great uplifter has the guts to admit that for some people the world may never be a friendly place.

Alone in Colt's Neck, Springsteen recorded at least 18 songs in late December and early January: the 10 songs that made up *Nebraska*; three songs that would make it to *Born in the U.S.A.* in different versions (the title cut, "Downbound Train," and "Workin' on the Highway," here called "Child Bride"); early versions of future *U.S.A.* B-sides "Johnny Bye Bye" and "Pink Cadillac"; "Losin' Kind," which has never been released; and the odd cover, most likely to test the equipment, like "Dream Baby" and "Precious Memories." (The *Nebraska* B-side, "The Big Payback," was cut later.)

Let's start with "Precious Memories," a version of the old hymn that became a country-gospel standard (it was once reported to be Gladys Presley's favorite song). No doubt Springsteen never intended to release "Precious Memories." It's of a piece with the ageless country music he was listening to at the time (everyone from Merle Haggard to Aretha Franklin had cut a version; Bob Dylan himself would assay one on the shaky '86 album *Knocked Out Loaded*). In Springsteen's 72-second attempt, he overdubbed himself into a one-man Louvin Brothers, offering harmonies and experimenting with the capabilities of the four-track recorder. Although just for personal consumption, "Precious Memories" has the timeless directness and stillness Springsteen was looking for in his new songs. It's the plainspoken template for *Nebraska*.

Nebraska is a record stuffed with death. The title track is told in the voice of mass murderer Charlie

Starkweather; "Johnny 99" ends with another convicted killer, more of an amateur than Starkweather, begging to be electrocuted; "Highway Patrolman" includes a violent act that may turn out to be a murder; "Reason to Believe" includes both a dead dog getting poked by a stick and an old man passing away "in a whitewash shotgun shack." Dead relationships are everywhere, too. "Used Cars" and "My Father's House" are haunted by the ghosts of relatives who might as well be dead, and in "Atlantic City," the narrator tells his lover, "Our luck may have died and our love may be cold," before delivering the punch line: "But with you forever I'll stay." Pretty much everyone on the record is desperate, like the guy driving without license or registration in "State Trooper," hoping he doesn't get pulled over but almost hysterical for some connection. The last lines of that song are "Hey somebody out there, listen to my last prayer/Hi ho silver-o deliver me from nowhere." These are not people you'd be comfortable inviting over for dinner.

The one exception is the character pegged as the hero of the record, Joe Roberts from "Highway Patrolman." He's a very good policeman with a no-good brother, and he sees in his brother Frankie a cracked mirror, a shadow representing what he could have been. Frankie went to Vietnam, Joe got to stay home. Frankie got to dance with Maria, Joe married her. To these ears, Joe Roberts is the one character on the record whom Springsteen loves. He gives Roberts the sweetest musical setting on the entire LP, and the most time to say his piece. But Roberts's key line about his relationship with Frankie—"I catch him when he's strayin', teach him how to walk that line"—is a lie he's telling himself or the guy on the barstool next to him. The song ends with Joe chasing Frankie's car after his brother has done something terrible, seeing a sign announcing the impending Canadian border, and pulling to the side of the highway. Why? "Man turns his back on his family, he ain't no friend of mine." In other words, because he can't confront his brother and whatever is going on between them, the hero Joe Roberts lets his brother go free so Frankie can harm again.

Almost every song on *Nebraska* pivots on such an impossible choice. The only happy song on the record, "Open All Night," a song so drenched in Chuck Berry that it quotes both "Wee Wee Hours" and "Too Much Monkey Business," is also the tale of a speed-fueled journeyman whose "boss don't dig me so he put me on the night shift/It's an all-night run to get back to where my baby lives." He needs the job and he needs the girl, so he's trying to maintain both, but at the end of the next-to-last verse, he's still "got three more hours but I'm covering ground." The song rushes by in less than three minutes, in a frenzy of words that makes "Blinded by the Light" seem relaxed in comparison. It's a song about feeling winded, sung in a way that leaves the singer nearly out of breath verse after verse. As Springsteen once wrote, "This song is very hard to perform."

It might be hard to perform physically, but other songs might have been more difficult to perform emotionally. "Mansion on the Hill" and "Used Cars" are presented as straight autobiography, angry and confused memories of a childhood without money or any evidence that dreams were worth having. The one literal dream documented on *Nebraska*, "My Father's House," ends on "this dark highway where our sins lie unatoned." And then there's "Reason to Believe." It's a list of why everything is broken—one woman imagines her long-gone daddy will one day return, another abandons her groom at the altar, another baptizes her son in a pointless exercise. In the midst of this, the narrator laughs at them. All this belief? It strikes him as funny. If Springsteen had tried to convey that sentiment with the grand accompaniment of the E Street Band, I wonder whether fans would have bounced The Artist Formerly Known as Rock'n'Roll Future back to rock'n'roll past rather quickly. Springsteen has never discussed this, but perhaps presenting this unexpected and unwanted thought—that there's no reason to believe—in an "experimental" context gave him cover. Maybe he didn't really mean it, some fans and critics wrote, thought, and hoped. (A similar misinterpretation could make "Atlantic City" sound pro-reincarnation.)

Even without the grand E Street Band, Springsteen's *Nebraska* is diverse musically, from the flat-out rock-'n'roll of "Open All Night" to the hush of the childhood memories in "Mansion on the Hill" and "Used

Cars." And, perhaps because the recordings were not intended for public consumption, *Nebraska* features the least mannered vocals of Springsteen's career, as if he's freed from worrying about what he would sound like to his audience. When he sings "Nebraska" in Starkweather's voice, he captures the flat bravado of the killer. Something similar happens in "Child Bride," later recast as "Working on the Highway" for *Born in the U.S.A.*, in which a jailed man tells his tale of busted love in a way that gets your sympathy until you realize he's a pedophile. Another leftover, "Losin' Kind," uses the same plainspoken voice to less effect. The only moment in the song that works is a gallows joke: After the narrator wraps his Buick around a telephone pole, the highway patrolman who was chasing him says he's glad to be alive. The singer replies that he'll think that over. (The bones of "Losin' Kind" would be taken up later, and more successfully, on "Highway 29" from *The Ghost of Tom Joad*.)

It's not just a new quiet voice that debuts on *Nebraska*. There's a new wild voice here, too. At the end of "State Trooper," after asking to be delivered, Springsteen lets out an unexpected shout, surprising the listener and maybe himself, follows it with another longer one, and then quickly fades the song to a conclusion, as if he's given away too much—or if he feels it's too close to what he does in rock'n'roll mode and he wants to drop this acoustic guitar already, head to a club, plug in, twist, and shout. Those shouts are the links between the songwriter and the King of the Jersey Clubs.

Just as *Nebraska* was a compulsive record to make (and choose to release in that form), Springsteen's jump to any stage within reach spoke of obsession as well. He just couldn't stop. Sometimes he'd even play with two bands in two clubs the same evening, driving from Freehold to Asbury Park to play "Long Tall Sally" for the second time that night. If that's not enough, this was about the time he started his workout marathons.

When I tell you he'd jump onstage with anybody, I mean it: hence his appearance with forgotten units like Billy Rancher and the Unreal Gods or Jimmy and the Mustangs. If you had even the slightest following on the Shore circuit and didn't host Springsteen at some point in '82 or '83, there was something wrong with you. Onstage at the Stone Pony or the Fast Lane in Asbury or the Brighton Bar in Long Branch or Clarence Clemons's short-lived Big Man's West in Red Bank, Springsteen would hardly ever call for his own songs. Every now and then he'd play "Jersey Girl" with the Xerox artists in Beaver Brown or the more impressive second-string E Streeters in John Eddie and the Front Street Runners. With Cats on a Smooth Surface he'd attack "Open All Night," "From Small Things (Big Things One Day Come)," and a new song called "On the Prowl." He'd also play "From Small Things" with Dave Edmunds, who, unlike Springsteen at that point, had actually gotten around to releasing a version of the

River outtake. Little more than a week after recording what would turn out to be *Nebraska*, he joined Nils Lofgren onstage. And when Clemons's strong soul band, the Red Bank Rockers, played its home base, he'd call for "Tenth Avenue Freeze-Out." Springsteen found pleasure, and maybe solace, in deliberately, gloriously dumb bar-band covers like "Wooly Bully," "Mony Mony," and "Twist and Shout." *Nebraska* let Springsteen be a songwriter and performer without having to be The Boss; all these club shows let him rock out without having to be an Artist.

Nebraska was a commercial retrenchment so Springsteen could expand artistically, but all these versions of "Lucille" and "Carol" added up to little more than an artistic holding pattern. He had grown as a songwriter since *The River* and he could still rock the house with the best of them. It was now time to cut a record that showcased both sides and brought them together.

Chapter 5

In Which I Almost Kill
Max Weinberg

Jerry Williams should have a mansion, but all he has is an attitude. He started as a fine soul writer and producer, got radicalized in the sixties, and started releasing delightful, bizarro records under his new professional name, Swamp Dogg. As I write this, he's threatening to publish a cookbook called *If You Can Kill It, I Can Cook It*. He cuts iconoclastic records when he feels like it or when someone is willing to pay him to record one. My favorite of his many fine albums is the chipper *Total Destruction to Your Mind*, although the one with him riding a giant rat on the album cover is pretty good, too. His best album title, without question, is *I'm Not Selling Out, I'm Buying In*.

Swamp Dogg, who's been associated with more different labels in his long career than George Clinton and Graham Parker combined, may get through the night by turning the dirty truth about the rock'n'roll business into a joke, but he has a point: If you plan to be a rock-'n'roll star, you'd better plan to sell out. A rock'n'roller before there was rock'n'roll, Robert Johnson was said to have sold out in the most blatant, Faustian way: his talent in exchange for his very soul. Back in the real world, the two greatest rock'n'roll singers, Elvis Presley and Rod Stewart, made similar deals. They watered down their massive talents, and jumped onto every stupid trend and opportunity dangled before them. Elvis ended up dead; Rod ended up singing standards, which is artistically the same thing.

Little in rock'n'roll has such a rich history as top-drawer artists selling out. The Beatles switched from leather jackets to suits and ties to get on the track for Ed Sullivan. Mick Jagger mumbled the words to "Let's Spend the Night Together" so the Rolling Stones could do the same. The Police, a pretty good band albeit not anywhere near the same level, dyed their hair blond to score a bubblegum commercial. Even so, sometimes great art results when performers sell out: Bob Dylan and the Band's magnificent '74 "comeback" tour was not built from artistic desire. Rather, David Geffen made Dylan an offer he couldn't refuse.

Who or what are these performers selling out to and what are they buying into? They're selling out something purely artistic, the only thing they truly own, even if it's as peripheral as what clothes they wear (the Beatles) or two words in a pop song (the Stones). They're getting fame, money, access to a mass audience. None of those are bad things necessarily; it's easy to argue that they're essential to maintaining a career in the music business. But the Beatles and the Stones were popular already and would have retained a good chunk of their growing popularity without cleaning up their acts. It wasn't so black and white for other bands who didn't happen to be great or generating adequate business. Some critics (including, I regret to admit, me) went hard after the Del Fuegos and the Long Ryders, among others, in the mid-eighties for "selling out" by filming beer commercials. But both bands were in deep debt when they signed those deals and those commercials kept their enterprises afloat for awhile. They weren't really in the music business anymore—they were in the advertising business—but at least the cash infusion kept them on the road doing what they wanted to do for longer than they would have otherwise. Would it have been more honorable if they had given up and gone to day jobs? It's a tough question.

It's not a tough question when you ask those already rolling in dough whether they should take more. You can't compare the plight of the Del Fuegos or the Long Ryders to stadium-filling bands like the Who, who accepted beer sponsorship money because, in the words of recovering alcoholic Pete Townshend, he couldn't possibly commit to an American tour without access to a private plane. The Del Fuegos and the Long Ryders were both tough little bands and they were both broke.

The beer companies preyed on them; these little bands were, in the end, victims. If they wanted to stay in the music industry, they felt, they had to sell out. They had no choice.

After releasing *Nebraska*, Bruce Springsteen had a choice. He would never take a dime in corporate sponsorship—separating him from such alleged icons of purity as Bob Dylan, the Clash, and U2—but in '82 and '83 he did have plenty of time to ruminate over how popular he wanted to be. He was privileged: He had control over which way he would go. The experience of recording and releasing those personal recordings was quite fulfilling to him, and he sought to replicate that experience on his next record. He wanted to make a band record this time—indeed, he had several songs he cut with the E Street Band when he was trying to get the *Nebraska* songs working that ranged from promising to outstanding—but after enjoying a nice dose of commercial success with *The River* (the album was Number One on the *Billboard* album chart for a month; "Hungry Heart," his first Top Twenty single, made it all the way to Number Five) he was wondering whether, perhaps, that was as far as he wanted to go in that lucrative direction. He was financially secure and he wasn't sure what he had to say to the E Street Band then and there. Why not strike out toward uncharted territory rather than even more mainstream success? It was almost too easy to continue doing the rock-star thing. It seemed more challenging to drive off without a map.

146

Wherever Bruce Springsteen is as you read this, he might still be contemplating that question, which in some ways defines his career. Since the early eighties, he's gone back and forth between pure artistic statements like *Nebraska* and *The Ghost of Tom Joad* and more frankly commercial enterprises like *Born in the U.S.A.* and (at last count) three live albums, two hits compilations, and four live or fan-souvenir DVDs. Every now and then a song born of commercial considerations would turn out to be art, like his contribution to Jonathan Demme's film *Philadelphia*. All but his crassest maneuvers have some artistic credibility. When Springsteen defines a project, the operative question seems to be whether it's meant to be Big or Little.

At first, Springsteen saw the follow-up to *Nebraska* as continuing in the Little vein. A mere four-track home-recording system yielded *Nebraska*, so Springsteen's minimal commercial concession for his next album was to go relatively high-tech and have an eight-track board installed in the garage of his second home in Los Angeles. There he recorded some strong individual songs like "Sugarland," "Shut Out the Light," and a faster version of "Johnny Bye Bye." As a group, these numbers were quiet, contemplative, overheard, insular, of a thematic piece with *Nebraska* but more fleshed-out musically. The expansion from four-track recording to eight-track recording allowed much more room for overdubbing guitars, keyboards, and a drum machine. As a group of songs, they didn't fit at all with the

147

rock'n'roll material cut in '82 ("Born in the U.S.A.," "Glory Days," and others were in the can already). Considered together, these home recordings were more a nod to the *Nebraska* method than a sense of what might come next, what might happen if *Nebraska*-quality songs were recorded with a full band. A track here or there might work, but they couldn't form the center of a band record. There was more noise on the fade of *Nebraska*'s "State Trooper" than all these songs combined. So, reluctantly, Springsteen returned to a New York studio with far more than eight tracks to work with (The Hit Factory, this time), reunited the band, and sought to figure out where he and the E Streeters should go next.

Not all of the E Streeters, though. Van Zandt was now officially (albeit quietly) departed, which had minimal impact on the arrangements but lowered Springsteen's comfort level. Van Zandt received a production credit for *Born in the U.S.A.* despite not being in on the '83 and '84 sessions. It's easy to argue that, with the possible exception of his delightfully ragged singing and mandolin playing on "Glory Days," Van Zandt's biggest contribution to the album was leaving. I don't mean this as a slight: Two songs on *Born in the U.S.A.*, "No Surrender" and "Bobby Jean," seem to be at least partly inspired by Van Zandt and his exit.

Born in the U.S.A. was the first Springsteen album that wasn't held together by a unifying idea. It shared with *The River* an attempt to capture both peaks and valleys, but nothing on it was as free as "Crush on You" or "I'm a Rocker." It shared with *Nebraska* plenty of dread and similar concerns, which shouldn't have been a surprise since more than half of *Born in the U.S.A.*, including the entire first side, emerged from the same '82 sessions during which the band wrestled with songs that ended up on *Nebraska*. But only "I'm on Fire" came out as pathological and scary as some of the numbers on *Nebraska* (a scariness that evaporated during a simultaneously silly and overly weighty promotional video). It didn't set out to be as extreme as either *The River* or *Nebraska*. With 12 songs, none of which hit the five-minute mark, this was a collection of short songs mostly intended for individual impact.

As with *The River*, those dozen songs on *Born in the U.S.A.* were the pick of many more that had been recorded, this time over the course of two years. (Max Weinberg guesstimated in a '84 interview with *Backstreets* that the band had cut 80 different songs over that time.) A quick listen to merely the small subset of outtakes that have appeared on B-sides or assorted compilations suggests a fine alternative album. "Murder Incorporated" was a bit overheated but captured the E Street Band at their most intense and hard-rocking. "This Hard Land" fulfilled Springsteen's dream of what an "electric *Nebraska*" might have sounded like: a big open sound, optimism tempered with realism, and a tough harmonica break. "Frankie" had been floating around since the '76 tour and was a link between the lengthy ballads of the seventies and the band's new, more streamlined approach. "None But the Brave" pointed back to that period, too, with a gorgeous guitar solo that arrived as a surprise. "Wages of Sin" was a downer, "Cynthia" organ-driven teenage rock, "Brothers Under the Bridges" recapitulated past triumphs (it sounded borrowed from *Born to Run*), "Rockaway the Days" looked back toward "Losin' Kind" and forward in the direction of *The Ghost of Tom Joad*'s "Straight Time," "Stand On It" and "TV Movie" were fun rockabilly workouts, "Pink Cadillac" drove across a sex metaphor with a tip to the *Peter Gunn* theme, "Car Wash" was a rare attempt to tell a tale of economic woe from the female point of view, "Janey Don't You Lose Heart" a sweet midtempo rocker, and "Man at the Top" a quiet song in which Springsteen acknowledged that, yes, he does want to be a superstar. Of the castoffs, the top to these ears remains "My Love Will Not Let You Down," a tough drums-and-guitar rocker that got worrisome at the end when an at-the-end-of-his-range Springsteen rasped, "Hold still now darling, hold still for God's sake," suggesting that whatever's going on here might not have been consensual.

Pick your favorites from those 15 and you end up with a double album that, cut for cut, can stand equal to *The River* in everything but thematic unity. There would have been repetition—"Brothers Under the Bridges" is too similar to "No Surrender," "Janey Don't You Lose Heart" apes "Be True," and a record in '84 with the rockabilly 1-2-3 of "Stand On It," "TV Movie," and "Pink Cadillac" should have come from the novelty revivalist trio Stray Cats, not the grand E Street Band. The impact of the album might have been diffused, too.

For those who like repetition, three songs in the middle of Side One told similar stories, in progressively more mournful tones. "Darlington County" has a sharp "Honky Tonk Women"—derived intro and, thanks to Van Zandt's I-am-Keith-Richards-I-am harmonies, it extended the sound of the easy rockers on *The River*. But beneath the giddiness, highway hypnosis, wordless choruses, and boasts (Clarence solo: all King Curtis and sugar, almost a parody of his "Big Man" sound), there was something disturbing rustling below the surface. Were the women they were propositioning prostitutes? When they arrive in Florida, the narrator and his friend end up on some work gang. As the narrator leaves Darlington County, he sees his road buddy "handcuffed to the bumper of a state trooper's Ford." It's unclear whether the Ford is moving. "Working on the Highway," an upbeat redo of the *Nebraska* castoff "Child Bride," again follows the narrator and his child bride down to Florida (where the authorities step in), this time ending with Wayne and the narrator swinging on a road gang.

The "up" tone of the song is similar to that of *Nebraska*'s "Johnny 99," more about the mania in the narrator's brain than a rational response to what's

151

going on around him. The beat slows down for "Down-bound Train," another song considered for *Nebraska*, featuring one of Weinberg's most fluid intro rolls. "Downbound Train" follows its narrator down down down as he loses his job, his girl, and his freedom. As has become commonplace for *Born in the U.S.A.* narrators, he ends up "swing[ing] a sledgehammer on a railroad gang." On these three songs, hopes vanish over and over, even when the music wants you to feel happy. Not surprisingly, on an album stuffed with hit singles, these three were among the mere five cuts from *Born in the U.S.A.* not extracted as 45s. The ballad that follows, "I'm on Fire," a tale of lust, loneliness, and maybe violence grafted atop a late-night Johnny Cash rhythm, was able to sneak all the way to Number Six on the pop chart.

Songs like "Darlington County" and "Working on the Highway" were meant to be ambiguous. You could dance and shout to them or you could wonder what was going on beneath all those "Sha-la-la's." Similarly, "Glory Days" slips some hard truths about aging into what first feels like a light performance. The album's opening track, the title number, turned out to be a lot more ambiguous than the songwriter intended. The version of "Born in the U.S.A." recorded as part of the *Nebraska* "sessions" laid out the story of the Vietnam veteran returning home to a country almost as unforgiving as the one he had just left. The performance was about only one thing: putting across the lyric. Future live acoustic versions of the song turned out bluesier and picked up some Eastern accents, but those were flourishes added to a song the audience knew by heart already. In this original acoustic demo, before there was any need to contextualize it, there were no thundering riffs, no pumping fists on the choruses, no 50,000 punters shouting along.

The full-band studio version of "Born in the U.S.A." made all that inevitable. Its airy sound—the first verse features only drums and synthesizer—led into one of the E Street Band's half-dozen most galvanic studio performances. It was an early take of the song, only the third time they'd played the song as a unit, and you can hear the band grab onto it with vigor. The lyrics in the verses were entirely unambiguous if you listened to them, but the anthemic music and the title of the song made it hard for many, from politicians to plebeians, to get to the lyrics—except for those of the chorus, which could be read many ways. But in the studio, long before anyone outside the band and crew heard it, "Born in the U.S.A." was hard, harsh, explosive. Springsteen wrote the song and sang the hell out of it, but the performance belongs to Weinberg's drums, as wild as Keith Moon's, as specific as Benny Benjamin's. Behind Weinberg, it's all texture: acoustic guitars, bass, and piano seem to be switching roles with the drums, offering a resilient foundation so the drums can fly.

The rhythms are what are really new on *Born in the U.S.A.* "Cover Me" was one of two songs Springsteen wrote for Donna Summer (she recorded and released the other one, "Protection"). Its skeetering guitar, minor-key arrangement, brittle beats, and lonely vocal yielded something very contemporary. *Born in the U.S.A.* is the first Springsteen record that sounds like the performer was listening to current pop radio when it was being made. There are throwbacks on *Born in the U.SA.*, like "No Surrender," which refers back to *Born to Run* in its wide-eyed arrangement and romantic lyrics, but *Born in the U.S.A.* is aggressively of-the-moment compared to earlier Springsteen records. It's not the sound of someone jumping onto the latest bandwagon à la Rod Stewart in "Da Ya Think I'm Sexy?"; instead, it's the sound of someone discovering, to his surprise, that his insular take on the world actually fits in with the world. Nowhere is that more apparent than "Dancing in the Dark."

All seven of the *Born in the U.S.A.* singles hit the Top Ten; the biggest smash was "Dancing in the Dark." It was written after producer Landau insisted that the album, which Springsteen claimed was finished, still needed a single, just as, more than a decade earlier, Columbia exec Clive Davis sent back the original version of *Greetings from Asbury Park, N.J.*, and told Springsteen the label wouldn't release the record until something more commercial was on it. Once again, Springsteen delivered. Buried on the second side of the album, after four songs that summoned The Ghost of E Street Past a bit more than any forward-looking record should, "Dancing in the Dark" crashed the party with the Sound of the New. As with "Born in the U.S.A.," "Dancing in the Dark" pushed forward on synthesizer and drums, but the two songs couldn't be more different in approach. Weinberg's drumming on "Dancing in the Dark" is the opposite of that on "Born in the U.S.A.," terse, all groove, and no "Mighty Max" flourishes or surprises. And unlike in "Born in the U.S.A.," this time Bittan's synthesizer stakes its position as lead instrument in the first second of the song and never relinquishes it. (There is plenty of electric guitar in the background, which suggests there may have been another way to present the song. It must have been an interesting mixing session.) It's a song about isolation and exhaustion ("I ain't got nothing to say," "I ain't nothing but tired," "I ain't getting nowhere"), but in the last verse you realize that the "you" in the song isn't some imagined audience but someone right there with him. "Hey baby!" he calls after the last chorus (Bruce Channel's song of that name is the likely reference) and Clemons's saxophone glides in with a massaging solo, offering the soundtrack for a lonely couple dancing together.

Springsteen, talking about "Dancing in the Dark," told Dave Marsh, "It was just like my heart spoke straight through my mouth, without even having to pass through my brain." He also wrote, in *Songs*, that the song "went as far in the direction of pop music as I wanted to go—and probably a little farther." The song did shoot him up from rock'n'roll star to full-fledged pop star, subject of everything from lifeless videos (he looks like a robot in the "Dancing in the Dark" promotional clip) to gossip columns. The only thing keeping it from the Number One spot was Prince's "When Doves Cry."

If you're going to be locked out of the crown by someone, it might as well be Prince, who was at his *Purple Rain* peak. Indeed, Springsteen and Prince were the twin kings of '84, releasing outstanding, challenging, complex records that sold in the millions, showing that, just as in the heyday of the Beatles, the Rolling Stones, and Bob Dylan, sometimes the best-selling records were indeed among the best. The mid-eighties was a heady time for pop music. Thanks to hip hop, Top Forty was revitalized. And in addition to Springsteen and Prince releasing career records, the airwaves were full of distinctive voices. Tina Turner had launched her thrilling comeback. Hell, even Don Henley made a handful of nonobnoxious records. That fluke of the moment got blown to smithereens rather quickly by realities ranging from Prince's next record, *Around the World in a Day*, being a psychedelic mess, to the jingoism that reigned that year in the United States as Reagan's reelection campaign fooled the electorate into thinking it was morning in America. The cynical among us might be content with the knowledge that the most culturally representative musical moment of '84 didn't have anything to do with Springsteen or

Prince. They'd say it took place in Los Angeles during the closing ceremonies of the pointless Summer Olympics. (Why pointless? Because the Soviet bloc countries boycotted and it felt like every medal ceremony gave the masses another chance to chant "U.S.A.") The '84 Olympics were feted afterward because they made money, which should tell you something about the way everything was judged. Anyway, at the closing ceremonies, Lionel Ritchie sang a "special" version of his treacly "All Night Long." As if that wasn't enough to turn the rest of the world against the United States, during the nighttime production sequence it was made to seem that aliens were landing in the middle of the stadium and Ritchie directed a new final verse to the "aliens." I haven't thought about this in many years, and 20 years later I'm still appalled. It was the sort of thing that made Up With People seem low-key. It was over-the-top and glitzy, the sort of thing rock'n'roll was invented to destroy. Prince and Springsteen were too ragged to define the center when there was still enough pop so bland in the center that only aliens might find it challenging.

If over-the-top was the zeitgeist, though, Springsteen was determined to meet it. If he felt his recorded version of "Dancing in the Dark" went deeper into pop music than he might have wanted, he went all the way down the rabbit hole with Arthur Baker's dance remixes of that song and two others for the omnipresent 12-inch singles. Baker was the top remixer at the time. His own

productions were the most exciting dance music—
"I.O.U." with Freez, "Planet Rock" and "Looking for
the Perfect Beat" with Afrika Bambaataa and Soul
Sonic Force, and many others—and he had even made
Cyndi Lauper sound funky with a smart rethink of her
signal hit "Girls Just Want To Have Fun." Tossing subtlety aside as he approached "Dancing in the Dark,"
Baker added layers of keyboards and percussion,
moved guitars up and down in the mix, pulled beats
tight until they snapped, and added his own electronic
rhythms. Atop all this, Springsteen's vocal was tugged
in many directions, sped up and thrown around on a
whim. Baker was a producer who respected the song
and the performer, but wouldn't let his fandom get in
the way of tearing the original track to the ground and
rebuilding it like a child with a Lego set and all the time
in the world. Baker pulled something angrier and
meaner out of "Dancing in the Dark" than Springsteen
intended and he did it in a clever way that should have
brought Springsteen a new audience. It didn't, some
diehard Springsteen fans were uncomfortable with it
(shades of "Disco Sucks"), and the three remix 12-inch
singles are, alas, out of print. We'll see them come out
of time capsules in 2084.

Twelve-inch singles, pop stars singing to aliens, and
MTV defined the world into which *Born in the U.S.A.*
was written, recorded, and released. The album became
a huge hit (Number One for seven weeks), followed by
single after single, and sellout arena shows turned into

sellout stadium shows. The concerts themselves were strong, but not different enough from '80–'81. Despite integrating two albums' worth of new material (there had been no *Nebraska* tour) and two new band members (guitarist Nils Lofgren and singer Patti Scialfa), the '84 tour felt an awful lot like its predecessor or, more specifically, like its predecessor on steroids. Springsteen's bulked-up physique was a metaphor for his show, full of grand gestures that ended up beating the audience into submission. The signposts were the same: "Thunder Road" ended the first set almost every night, as did "Rosalita" with the second set. Eventually even Springsteen tired of "Rosalita" and tried several songs in its slot, among them "Racing in the Street," which had grown a ridiculous spoken section. The encores would flow from "Born to Run" into a group of uptempo covers, many of which had been standard material on earlier tours. For an evening filled with new players and new music—the first performance of the tour found room for 13 songs from *Nebraska* and *Born in the U.S.A.*—it felt like the band was retracing its steps. Everything was bigger, especially in '85, when the tour moved to stadiums. But even on those nights when they took their new songs to strange, exciting new places ("Born in the U.S.A." grew a sharp guitar solo, for example) it often seemed like the band was a step behind the new image. They may have been having the time of their lives and felt on top of the world, but they weren't going many new places, at least not musically. They were doing what they did bigger and maybe better some nights, but most of the crowd was so far away that they were looking at video screens, not the stage. I'm not making the purist's argument here that stadiums are bad and bands are inevitably distanced from their audience or their muses or something when they head for the open air. The E Street Band's tremendous run of stadium shows at the end of the *Rising* tour in the fall of '03 is ample evidence to the contrary. What I am arguing is that an arena set list has to be rethought when brought into the great outdoors, and Springsteen did not do that. Springsteen had become a star beyond anyone's expectations and the attention seemed distracting some nights. How ubiquitous was Springsteen? Rick Springfield (*General Hospital*, "Jesse's Girl") wrote a song about being mistaken for Springsteen and that complaint was a hit. Springsteen was offered a reported $12 million to sing for General Motors (he turned it down) and two presidential candidates claimed he supported them (he endorsed neither). The *National Enquirer*, which would one day have other Springsteen news to report, ran a piece under the headline "I Want To Be the Next Governor of New Jersey."

Springsteen responded to his massive fame and its ramifications by going philanthropic (he gave away what seemed like millions), looking to build a personal life (a short-lived marriage to a model/actress), and, after a 16-month tour, compiling and cashing in with the live album fans had been clamoring for since the

Main Point days, the five-LP *Live 1975/85*, which came out amid huge fanfare in November '86. It was a sizeable hit, preceded by such hype that hour-plus first-day lines at record stores were reported.

Note the lifeless cover photo. Springsteen looks like he belongs at Madame Tussaud's—and if the boxed set is credited to "Bruce Springsteen and the E Street Band," why is he the only guy pictured? Acknowledge several key omissions, particularly "Prove It All Night," a high point almost every night from '78 to '85. Moan a bit that the set doesn't acknowledge the Sancious/Carter era. Other than that, *Live 1975/85* offers little to complain about. It serves up more than three hours of music with minimal fluff. Some of the long intros and speeches ("The River") could have ended on the outtake reel without losing much, but that's about it. OK, it's misnamed: It's virtually *Live 1978/85*, since only the first of its 40 performances, a solo "Thunder Road," was performed in '75. Without attempting to mirror the structure of an actual show, the live box proceeds in mostly chronological order, taking listeners through the growth of the band. The set peaks in its second half: The 17 consecutive entries from '84 and '85 capture many of the finest moments of the *Born in the U.S.A.* tour and represent it as better than it actually was.

The '78 songs were recorded in clubs or theaters. The "Adam Raised a Cain" is primal, the version of "Fire" is mean-spirited enough to have caught the attention of the National Organization for Women (not

a joke), and "Paradise by the 'C'" remains a sharp
Shore instrumental, the archetypal sound of summer.
For '80 and '81, we're listening to the band in arenas
and at first the fade-up sound of the larger crowd is
exciting even before the music starts. The band doesn't
always try to fill every nook and cranny of the big halls.
On the '84–'85 versions of "Nebraska," "Johnny 99,"
and "Reason to Believe," you can hear the echo and the
enormous space around the small sound. The band does
little to muscle up those *Nebraska* songs for arenas and
stadiums: Bass and drums help out a bit, a touch of percussion and keyboard add color, but the songs are still
miniatures. You have to lean forward to hear. And
when the band does aim to make every inch of the Los
Angeles Coliseum count, they grab Edwin Starr's
"War" by the throat and fill the sky.

Roughly two-thirds through the box, there are
"Born in the U.S.A." and "Seeds," part of the four-song
tape Jon Landau sent Springsteen at the end of the tour
supporting *Born in the U.S.A.*, suggesting "we might
have something here" (the other two were "The River"
and "War"). You can hear in those two songs what was
strongest about the stadium half of the *Born in the
U.S.A.* tour. The shows started with a martial "Born in
the U.S.A." It takes a leap of imagination to believe
Springsteen could launch a show by singing this hard
and keep going for three more hours. "Seeds," which
follows, was a new song debuted on the European leg
of the tour and was a regular part of the set for the U.S.

stadium run. It was a perfect everynighter for the summer spent crossing Reagan's America, a hard-rock illustration of why it wasn't morning in America but closer to 11:59 p.m. Over a Z.Z. Top riff (the E Street Band was familiar with those, since Springsteen called for "I'm Bad, I'm Nationwide" every now and then) that gave the song a tough electric *Nebraska* feel, Springsteen chewed over the tale of a family that drives south to Houston looking for work, finds none, and suffers the sort of indignities the Okies experienced in real life and the film version of *The Grapes of Wrath* that Springsteen so admired. But this is not a song written in broad strokes, as John Steinbeck's novel and John Ford's film were. It's the small details, like one of the narrator's children suffering from a "graveyard cough," that gives the song power. The song ends with the narrator so broke he doesn't even have spit to spare, warning others not to follow him down: "You're better off buying a shotgun dead off the rack."

At the peak of his fame, at one of the peaks of the career of any rock'n'roll star, when he had a Number One album that yielded more Top Ten singles than any had before, when he could sell out six stadium shows in his home market and multiple nights elsewhere, when presidential candidates and political commentators were arguing over who owned him, with "Seeds" Springsteen was struggling to continue doing what got him in that position. He returned to the method he developed while writing the songs for *Darkness on the*

Edge of Town and stuck with since: tell accurate, unflinching stories of the people who weren't as lucky as he was. As he looked out at the vast stadium crowds, he must have known those were the people filling the stadiums. They still needed to see a reflection of themselves onstage; Springsteen still needed to deliver that. No one else in the crowd was a millionaire guitar player who got to shake his ass in front of 60,000 people every night and then go back to a five-star hotel with his model/actress wife. If all the audience saw was a star, the whole thing would have come tumbling down and Springsteen might as well have taken the $12 million or whatever it was from General Motors.

You could feel all this coming as the *Born in the U.S.A.* tour started in June '84 in St. Paul, Minnesota. The attention the new record was getting was more than ever before (although tickets for opening night were available for face value from scalpers outside the Civic Centre). It was as if everything on the commercial side had finally fallen into place, without artistic compromises to get there. Even side projects released by band members at the time were considered noteworthy. Along with writer Robert Santelli, Max Weinberg had just published *The Big Beat: Conversations with Rock's Great Drummers*, a collection of fun, entertaining interviews with many of Weinberg's heroes. My favorite moment comes toward the end of the book, during a talk with the Rolling Stones' Charlie Watts, during which Weinberg and Watts, the two greatest white drummers of the rock'n'roll era, found themselves talking about another giant, Hal Blaine, whom Watts befriended during an early Stones tour of the United States. "He was a lovely man," Watts remembered. "He had the first remote-controlled garage door opener I'd ever seen."

I was in St. Paul for two reasons: To witness the start of the tour and to interview Weinberg for a music magazine that has long departed. After the interview, he invited me to join him for lunch at a local mall, after a book signing. I met him at the book store, where 50 or so people brought him a book or an LP to sign (one offered up the "Dancing in the Dark" 12-inch for a signature; he laughed, graciously), and after lunch I offered him a ride back in my rental car (they were out of compacts at the airport, so I wound up with a blue Lincoln Continental) along with two of my friends. I promptly got lost, finding a 45-minute extremely indirect way back to the hotel that was only 20 minutes away. I remember two U-turns; there may have been more. I was nervous. I was a young professional writer who had conducted an informative interview, but I was also a fan at the wheel of an unfamiliar vehicle. My nervousness over that, coupled with my frustration that all my driving didn't appear to get me any closer to the hotel, led me to run a red light. We didn't come close to hitting another car or being hit by another car, but the rest of the ride was quiet and awkward. I was embarrassed, as I suppose were my buddies.

I hadn't thought much about that for many years, until I began writing the essay that included the *Born in the U.S.A.* era and it all came back to me, with far more emotion than I felt at the time. I promptly imagined the worst. What if we had been hit by a car, hard, and Weinberg had been injured, killed even, and the tour would be over, the E Street Band would be over, and I would be the most hated person in the world? (To prove that I still have the unfinished brain of an adolescent, I failed to consider the possibility that two of my closest friends would be dead, too, not to mention me.) In that brief, irrational worry, it hit me how much the E Street Band means to so many people, how lucky we are to have them, be they several blocks away on a stadium face or 10 feet away in an overstuffed club.

Speaking of overstuffed clubs, around the time the live box came out, Springsteen showed he could switch between Big and Little at whim. Most of the E Street Band played a brief, shtick-free, intense set at the Stone Pony in support of a 3M plant in Springsteen's hometown Freehold, about to be closed down. He accepted an invitation from Neil Young and performed a solo set at Young's annual Bridge Concert at the Shoreline Amphitheater in Mountain View, California. With occasional backing from Federici and Lofgren, Springsteen opened with a strange, a capella "You Can Look (But You Better Not Touch)" and used his hour to bring his sound, his career, and himself back down to human size. "Born in the U.S.A.," "Darlington County," and especially "Dancing in the Dark" lost their studio gloss (with the synth riff transferred to Federici's accordion and Lofgren's acoustic guitar, "Dancing in the Dark" sounded like a rockabilly blues), "Seeds" lost its Z.Z. Top riff and came across as pure anger. Springsteen was having a good time on "Hungry Heart" and other light songs, but he was intent on not being The Boss. Even when he engaged in some rock-star posing, as on the version of "Fire" that you can see on the *Anthology* video-compilation disc, he made it very clear he knew that such posturing was a joke.

That esthetic ruled as Springsteen turned inward and wrote the songs that would yield *Tunnel of Love* ('87), a spare, harrowing, seductive tour through domestic life in all its intricate glory and messiness. He wrote the songs quickly and, after a pair of false starts in studios on either coast, brought the recording process home and kept the recording as personal as the songs themselves. This time the studio wasn't the four-track of *Nebraska* or the eight-track of the "Hollywood Hills" demos for *Born in the U.S.A.* A full-fledged 24-track digital recording studio now resided on Springsteen's New Jersey property.

What Springsteen didn't do was cut the record with the E Street Band. Every member of the band got a credit, but barely, as they were called in to overdub their parts after Springsteen recorded the basic tracks himself. Only Weinberg contributed to more than three of the record's dozen cuts, and that was because he was

167

brought in to replace the metronomic click track. This was a solo album with coloring supplied by reliable collaborators, but there was none of the give-and-take, searching, or lengthy sessions you'd associate with a full-fledged E Street Band endeavor. Brief indeed: Only five extra recordings from the sessions have emerged, and only one of them—"The Wish," a piece of naked autobiography in which Springsteen lays out how much he owes his mother—was album-worthy. "Lucky Man" and "Two for the Road" earned their status as B-sides; "When You Need Me" and the slight, homespun "Honeymooners" came out on *Tracks*. All were solo recordings. Except for a few days at the Hit Factory in '95 to record some new songs (and to rerecord some unreleased songs) to fill out *Greatest Hits*, *Born in the U.S.A.* turned out to be the last time the E Street Band recorded a full studio album together until *The Rising* ('02). Lofgren and Scialfa were part of the band for nearly 20 years before they got to participate in a full studio set. Springsteen had now recorded two of his last three studio records bandless. At least as a recording artist, Springsteen had gone solo. As he wrote in his brief liner notes to *Greatest Hits*, "after '85 I'd had enough."

Tick, tick, tick. That's the sound at the heart of *Tunnel of Love*. Although Springsteen had a full 24-track studio at his disposal, the dozen cuts on the album often come back to a lonely man wrestling with time, which, apologies to Martin Amis, is only headed in one direction. The song on the album that's most literally about time, both lyrically and musically, is "One Step Up," a ballad that chronicles time passing and its associated deterioration. In one verse, a busted furnace and a dead engine are metaphors for the unhappiness filling their house; in another verse, the narrator is in transition in a hotel; in yet another, he's in a bar considering a pickup and fantasizing about the woman he may have left behind. The quiet singing, the plaintive details (the narrator ponders a bird outside his motel room, the presence or absence of a wedding ring) make it feel like you're right inside the singer's heart. The rhythms are soothing but the message isn't. You're with the singer, he's desperate to connect, he has someone he's connected with but can't anymore, he dreams of holding his wife but can't figure out how to. When the E Street Band played the song live on their '88 tour, the cold ending (it fades on disc) felt like time running out. "I wanna know if love is real," from "Born to Run," is said to be the line that encapsulates Springsteen's career. Love can be real, of course, but it's not for most of the characters on *Tunnel of Love*. Only on "Tougher Than the Rest," "All That Heaven Will Allow," and perhaps the closing waltz "Valentine's Day" is there any assurance that the relationship will continue after the song ends. The wisest and most moving song on the album is the most modest, "Walk Like a Man," the sound of a man, on his wedding day, finally comprehending the meaning of his father's life. "So much has happened to

169

me/That I don't understand," the narrator says, once again a boy trying to be worthy of his father. It's worth pointing out that nowhere in the song is the narrator thinking about his bride on their wedding day. In terms of subject, the record represented a huge jump in Springsteen's lyrics. Before *Tunnel of Love*, Springsteen had written more credible songs about his love for Steve Van Zandt ("No Surrender," "Bobby Jean") or some car than any family or romantic partner.

Like his Bridge show, Springsteen started off *Tunnel of Love* in a capella mode, with "Ain't Got You," snapping fingers to keep time, then constructing a one-man skiffle band that puts across the song—both boast and plaint, it would have been a great Elvis vehicle—with a light Bo Diddley beat. It's homemade and spare, but except for the title number it's the most complicated entry on the record. "Tunnel of Love," with its modern synthesized introduction and its layers of vocals, effects, and keyboards, ending in the sound of a family riding on a New Jersey roller coaster, was the most "produced" song on the set. Lyrically, it was built on an old metaphor picked up by countless filmmakers and songwriters. Dire Straits had used it most recently in their song of the same title. Its propulsive polyrhythms (all sorts of percussion collide) convey a story of indecision and fear. Each stop on the carnival ride is another chance for disaster: "The lights go out and it's just the three of us/You and me and all that stuff we're so scared of." The music keeps shifting as the ride goes on; Arthur Baker would have had a gas blowing up this one.

He should have gotten a shot, because no one else on this record sounds like he or she is having much fun. "Two Faces" is very close to Lou Christie's '63 hit "Two Faces Have I" (Christie was a master at conveying conflicting urges and emotions, especially on "Lightnin' Strikes"). It's a tale of a man listening to conflicting advice from an angel on one shoulder and the devil on the other, ending with the narrator, saying of the dark half trying to ruin his life, "go ahead and let him try," which should sound defiant and victorious, except it's followed immediately by a taunting organ solo, saying "nyah-nyah" to the boast. There's trouble in the bedroom of "Brilliant Disguise," too. The first single from the album, it cruises in a semi-Latin feel suggestive of the Drifters (listen hard and you'll hear the tympani), supporting the story of someone "Struggling to do everything right/And then it all falls apart." (Note to narrator: It probably would have been a good idea not to have been married by that gypsy.) It's the most traditional-E-Street-Band-sounding entry on the record, thanks especially to Roy Bittan's melodic piano. The line Springsteen goes out on summarizes the album neatly: "God have mercy on the man who doubts what he's sure of." Have mercy on him when he doesn't doubt it, too: The kiss-off "When You're Alone" is one of the most hard-hearted songs in the Springsteen catalogue.

It's the only time on the album that the band sings along; the irony feels intentional.

Only two of the songs on *Tunnel of Love* leapt from first-person narrative to omniscient observation and they couldn't have been more different. With nods to country and blues but still rocking out, "Spare Parts" details what happened after "Bobby said he'd pull out/Bobby stayed in." That's the only reference to sex on an album about mostly romantic relationships. Many of these characters on the album are so estranged from the physical that sex is either a memory or a far-away goal, something they'd like to try again after they get their act together and feel comfortable in the presence of another person. Or themselves. Springsteen aims for a severe Flannery O'Connor feel with a visionary last verse, in which Janey, the woman abandoned by Bobby, hears of a woman in a neighboring town who delivered her baby to the local river, Moses style. Janey brings her baby to the riverside, thinks better of the example, carries him home, and goes downtown to pawn her engagement ring and wedding dress. You can almost hear the narrator chuckle that at the end of every hard-earned day people find some reason to believe.

On the other hand, "Cautious Man" is a song about a man who has "LOVE" tattooed on one hand and "FEAR" on the other (it's left ambiguous whether this is metaphorical or literal). Softly, it's the story of "an honest man" who "wanted to do what was right" but feels adrift; Springsteen has traced this character back to "Stolen Car" from *The River*, someone who just can't fit in, the adult version of a lonely teenager who sits on the edge of his bed, bent over his guitar, hoping the chords he's practicing will lead to a better life. Bill Horton, the character in the song, is the same guy in "Two Faces" at a moment of greater indecision. He's afraid to do anything because he knows he's going to do the wrong thing. That fear takes a rare toll on Springsteen the lyricist, too. Renowned as a ruthless editor of his own material, here he lets "Cautious Man" go on a verse too long. The song feels like it's ending with "He got dressed in the moonlight and down to the highway he strode/When he got there he didn't find nothing but road," showing how the romance of the highway is a dead end. In the verse after that, Springsteen settles for a deus ex machina ending, "God's fallen light" doing the job that specific writing is supposed to. It was a rare misstep on a tight, entirely coherent set of related songs that took Springsteen somewhere new as a songwriter, something superstars don't often permit themselves to do.

Springsteen considered how best to present these hushed songs to his audience in person and decided that taking them on the road with the E Street Band was the answer. Dubbed the "Tunnel of Love Express," it was a tour intended to disorient. It made the band ill at ease. Most of them were asked to perform in different areas on the stage than they had since the early seventies, and a long ramp in the middle of the stage led up to a crack horn section drawn from the Asbury Jukes. Surprising, considering *Tunnel of Love* was so small-scale, this was the most showy, choreographed stage set yet for the E Street Band. Songs didn't change much from night to night. "Rosalita," now exiled to the encores, was beginning its slide into retirement, and "Born to Run" was performed solo acoustically by Springsteen, although he didn't have the stage to himself. He made sure the band stood beside him as he cut that anthem down to human size. The new second-set closer was a bit of roadhouse, "Light of Day," the song Springsteen wrote as a consolation prize to Paul Schrader after he had stolen the title of the director's film to use as the title of *Born in the U.S.A.*

It was a bizarre tour. Especially during the first three shows, in Worcester, Massachusetts, you could see the band members standing close to their marks, concerned like they didn't know where they were in relation to one another as if the best way not to bump into anything or anyone was to stay put. Gary Tallent slicked his hair back like a rockabilly cat, maybe so it would be easier for others on the stage to see him and stay clear. The entrance was a gimmick: band members came out one by one, taking tickets from a carnival barker, picking up their part of the "Tunnel of Love" intro, the last member being Springsteen, who would invite the audience on a date or a ride, throw roses at them, and then call for the song proper. The horns added a soul kick when they entered before the final verse, and they filled in songs both old and new, not only the warhorses you'd expect, but also less-worn numbers like the rough "Adam Raised a Cain." But the set also included plenty of synchronized dancing (during the never-before-played-live rockabilly arrangement of "You Can Look [But You Better Not Touch]") and a long set piece during which Springsteen and Clemons sat on a park bench. That was a low point. Some of the highs were the end of the first set, a double shot of "War" going right into a blockbuster "Born in the U.S.A." that ensured that any ambiguity was entirely a construction of a willful listener, and two new songs in the second set. "I'm a Coward" was a light soul rocker, built from pieces of Gino Washington's "Gino Is a Coward," that for its length was able to turn fear of intimacy, one of the themes of *Tunnel of Love*, into a joke.

"Part Man Part Monkey" was the only reggae song I know of that both mentions the Scopes trial and includes a snatch of Mickey and Sylvia's "Love Is Strange." The lyrics range from the monkeys of the Scopes trial ('25, teacher tried for teaching evolution, might happen again in '05 America) to the monkey suit on a groom to the monkey inside all men. It's more carnal than *Tunnel of Love* and would have fit in well there. As the man himself said introducing the song at a widely bootlegged northern California show: "There's thems that believe we came from Adam and Eve, and then there's thems that, um, like this."

175

New songs, check. New choreography, check. What about new roles? The tour offered one of those as well. Backup singer Patti Scialfa was playing a much larger role onstage, usurping the Van Zandt-Lofgren sidekick responsibility, sharing the front-center mic with The Boss far more than in the previous tour. The second set of these shows usually opened with the austere, devotional "Tougher Than the Rest," a downtempo but upbeat presentation, full of laconic guitar, of the promises that filled songs like the then-still-unreleased "My Love Will Not Let You Down." At the same microphone, their mouths inches from one another, Springsteen and Scialfa dueted this profession of love looking straight at one another. It's pointless to confuse art with real life, but you didn't have to be the *National Enquirer* to realize that something was going on. Their relationship went public eventually. Despite trying to undercut his fame by not releasing some sort of *Born Again in the U.S.A.* record, Springsteen had photographers tracking and pinpointing exactly when he stopped wearing his wedding ring onstage.

As the European leg of the tour wound down, Springsteen announced that he and the band were joining the Amnesty International Human Rights Now! Tour, a multiperformer caravan intended to raise awareness about the 40th anniversary of the United Nations Declaration of Human Rights, a bold document regularly cited and ignored by governments all over the planet. Over six weeks, the tour stopped at 20 cities on four continents. The core lineup was Youssou N'Dour, Tracy Chapman, Peter Gabriel, Sting, and Springsteen, with local performers joining in on many occasions. There was plenty of interplay between the bands. Every night they'd perform Bob Marley's "Get Up, Stand Up" and Bob Dylan's "Chimes of Freedom" en masse, and each performer showed up during other performers' sets. Sting would regularly sing "The River" with the E Street Band, sometimes along with L. Shankar, the violinist in Gabriel's band. Another member of Gabriel's troupe was former E Street keyboardist David Sancious, who had a chance to play again with his old boss.

Let me begin this paragraph praising Sting by mentioning that I think the guy and his music are insufferable. He did some fine work as part of the Police, but his solo career has been a lurch from one pretentious jazz-pop nadir to another. If you love somebody, shut the hell up. When I attended the Human Rights Now! show in Montreal in September '88, I was prepared to eat or talk during his set. Yes, he did his usual meandering pieces in which he made the world safe for his ego, but he did something else as well. Witnessing Springsteen's set during the previous seven shows, he decided that rocking out might not be beneath him. His uptempo songs were more spirited than usual and the improvisations that extended them, led by Branford Marsalis, were exceptional. The last song he played that night was the best song he'll ever write, the

Police standard "Every Breath You Take," which he sang as a duet with Springsteen. "Every Breath You Take" is a rarity in the Sting canon, a deeply felt pop song, but also a deceptively complex love song with a sinister aftertaste. The two took on "Every Breath You Take," with great feeling, never oversinging, getting inside the song, Sting's band (augmented by E Streeters Bittan, Clemons, and Lofgren) rising with them, never rushing, pushing deeper, as the joy of the performance held sway over the paranoia of the lyrics. It's one of the most controlled and elegant performances of either man's career. They left the stage arm in arm.

It's good that Springsteen was making rock-star friends, because he was at the end of his rope with the E Street Band. He was hardly making records with them anymore and had quickly grown closer with one member of the band than he could ever be with any of the others. Asking them to stand in different places was symptomatic of a larger problem: Springsteen worried about it before, but this time he really did not know where to put the E Street Band anymore. They could play strong, sometimes soaring, live shows together. There's no one alive with whom he could better play nearly all of his songs. But he wasn't writing songs with them in mind anymore. For the Amnesty tour, they reverted to an abbreviated version of their *Born in the U.S.A.* tour set (they played "Brilliant Disguise" occasionally, but that was it from his most recent album), because, with few exceptions, the songs on *Tunnel of*

Love did not represent what made the E Street Band such a force of nature on a concert stage. Everything was up in the air. It was time for a change or at least a break. So in late '89, Springsteen let the members of the E Street Band know that he was going to try something else for a while. As Nils Lofgren said at the time, "He's allowed to be confused."

Chapter 6

Hollywood

As far as quality goes, few mainstream rockers have had a run like Van Morrison enjoyed in the early 70s. *Moondance, His Band and Street Choir, Tupelo Honey, St. Dominic's Preview,* the live *It's Too Late To Stop Now,* and *Veedon Fleece* were all full of strange and wondrous music, Celtic rhythm-and-blues with horns that could blow down the walls of a city and words that either expressed profound thoughts or melted into roaring and scatting as Morrison hunted for a place beyond words, a peaceful home safe from the tyranny of language. He never did find it for long, but that didn't stop his bloodhound search. Only *Hard Nose the Highway* from that period hasn't lasted: From '70 to '74 Van the Man batted .857.

Tupelo Honey stood apart from the rest of those classics, though, because of its tone. Aside from "Wild

Night," in which Morrison's voice sounded sad despite the song being an invitation to a party, it was a genuinely happy record, and happiness is not an emotion fans have come to associate with Van Morrison records. The gnome almost smiles on the LP's inner sleeve, one of three photos of him in the album package, all accompanied by partner Janet Planet (she sells jewelry over the Internet nowadays, in case you were wondering). Granted, the other tinted photo in the package looks like it escaped from *Wisconsin Death Trip*, but here the corners of Morrison's mouth are dangerously close to turning up.

Tupelo Honey is full of winning celebrations, but it's a record that's hard to trust compared to his others of the time. Morrison made his career on albums like *Astral Weeks*, with songs of doubt, insecurity, and all sorts of anguish. When he delivers an album with his pictures of his beloved beside him and song titles like "You're My Woman," it's easy to be suspicious. Rock-'n'roll is not music about being satisfied; it's music about shouting that you can't get no satisfaction. The most telling albums about love tend to be those like *Tunnel of Love* or Richard and Linda Thompson's *Shoot Out the Lights*, records more about complexity than happy endings. No one listens to John and Yoko's recorded lovefests to listen to what a relationship feels like; they go to something more pointed like "I'm Losing You." Happiness can fuel great pop music, from "I Feel Good" to "Shiny Happy People," "Whole Lotta

Shakin' Going On" to "Crazy in Love," "Rosalita" to "Out in the Street." Anyone who's grown up a rock-'n'roll fan connects art with yearning, be it romantic, spiritual, political, economic, or otherwise. What was untrustworthy about *Tupelo Honey* was its lack of yearning. Van Morrison, the guy who let you feel what it was like to watch a lover die or sit in a car staring at someone you love but can never possess, was now singing domestic bromides. It was as out of character as, say, Prince becoming a Jehovah's Witness and refusing to curse or sing sexually explicit lyrics anymore: Who could believe something like that could ever happen?

Around '90, Bruce Springsteen realized he was happy, realized he could be happy, and emerged from whatever he had been struggling with for years. All those songs about men who had no clue how to behave in relationships; he couldn't have been making them all up. But the public Springsteen was more the man he wanted to be than the private one. "I went out in '85 and talked a lot about community," Springsteen told Jim Henke in *Rolling Stone* in '92, "but I wasn't part of any community." By '90, he and Scialfa were parents, and the time he spent out of the limelight was a chance for him to woodshed personally, if not musically.

Whatever happened behind closed doors during those years paid off. The Springsteen who emerged—briefly in November '90 for a pair of acoustic benefit concerts and then more emphatically in April '92 with the release of two albums of new material, *Human*

Touch and *Lucky Town*—was a confident man. He hadn't released an album of new material in half a decade and he wanted to return Big. So big, indeed, that he decided to split his 22 new songs between two separate records (Guns N' Roses had recently pulled off a similar trick with two buy-'em-one-at-a-time volumes of *Use Your Illusion*). *Human Touch*, recorded with L.A. session men, was intended as the follow-up to *Born in the U.S.A.*, aimed at the mainstream; *Lucky Town*, cut mostly in his home studio, was the new *Tunnel of Love*, but this time with louder sounds and better news to report.

Three of the songs from *Human Touch* (as well as three others that didn't make the cut) debuted during two acoustic benefits Springsteen performed for the Christic Institute in November '90. It was a high-profile appearance after two years of a very low profile, rarely (comparatively) showing up at clubs, and having spent nearly a year locked in various studios figuring out what he wanted to write about. It was time to come up for some air.

Springsteen's music may have defined the rock'n'roll mainstream for many, but the cause for which he picked up his guitar was far more fringe. The Christic Institute was best known for its work investigating Iran/contra drug-running connections, some quite real, and it should be pointed out that the organization was an early critic of the illegal excesses committed in the name of the U.S. government in Central America in the eighties. However, the Christic Institute also flirted with some easily discredited far-right conspiracy theories, which led to its being disowned by those few remaining on the rational left (Chip Berlet's work for Political Research Associates documents this definitively). Onstage at the Shrine Auditorium in Los Angeles, Springsteen mentioned the reason for the concerts only briefly, dedicating one of his new songs, "When the Lights Go Out," to "the people of the Christic Institute, who watch what's going on when the lights go out." During those performances, especially the first night, it's clear that what was on Springsteen's mind was not a government watchdog group but himself. He walked onstage in faded jeans, his shirt tail hanging out. Before he played his first song, he said, "It's been a while since I did this, so if you're moved to clap along—please don't." He sounded particularly nervous during the first song, "Brilliant Disguise," but when he switched from guitar to piano midway through the set (to assay a nostalgic "Tenth Avenue Freeze-Out"), he joked, "any bad notes are intentional." His performance gathered strength as the evenings progressed, with a set list that reached back as far as "Wild Billy's Circus Story" and looked forward with the carnal "Red Headed Woman," which he dedicated to both Scialfa and Bonnie Raitt, one of the other performers that evening. "Red Headed Woman" is funny, devotional, direct: Springsteen may be the first rock'n'roller who had to settle down before he could write a good song about sex.

185

Spirited and soulful covers of Dylan's "Highway 61 Revisited" and "Across the Borderline" (by Ry Cooder, John Hiatt, and Jim Dickinson) with Raitt and Jackson Browne closed the show both nights and served as the end of a modest, friendly return to the concert stage. At the time, the response to the performances verged on the messianic, and for a time there was talk of releasing the concerts as a record or video. Wiser heads prevailed: More than three years after the release of *Tunnel of Love*, yet another live album focusing on catalogue material would have cemented the image of Springsteen, now 41, as someone past his prime, looking back at past triumphs and trying to use the new "Unplugged" vehicle as a way to stretch some more life out of those warhorses. And even a cursory listen to the new songs debuted at the Christic reveals that, despite how delighted Springsteen and his legions were that he was putting new music out there, they weren't that great.

In their defense, I should add that there was one thing no one knew yet: The Christic versions of these songs were far superior to what Springsteen would cut in various studios with a full band, which leads us to something we should be amazed took nearly 20 years to happen: a bad album by Bruce Springsteen. "*Human Touch* began as an exercise to get myself back into writing and recording," Springsteen wrote in *Songs*. These were genre exercises, not full-grown, organic songs, which should have been his hint to never release any of it. In his first attempt to build a band record without the E Street Band, unable to write songs that engaged him, Springsteen set out on a variety of exercises. He wrote a bunch of soul songs. He wrote a bunch of pop songs. He wrote songs built around bass lines. He didn't know what he wanted to write about, so he figured some structure would get him where he wanted to go. It didn't. It was only when E Street Band piano player Roy Bittan visited and played some pieces of music he was working on that Springsteen came to life, offering to write lyrics for the tracks and inviting Bittan to join the production team of the new record. So what got Springsteen going in his first band record away from the E Street Band, the record that was going to prove he could be a rock'n'roller without them? A member of the E Street Band.

Human Touch is a boring record by a rock star. Its sound is shiny, its lyrics are generic, its songs are often as clichéd as their titles ("Human Touch," "Cross My Heart," "Roll of the Dice," "All or Nothin' at All"), and the band members, such as they are, sound too focused on following instructions (or replicating the demos Springsteen and Bittan had cut) to internalize the songs. The core group for the album, aside from Springsteen and Bittan, was drummer Jeff Porcaro, the late studio stickman best-known for his years spent trying to sneak a little rhythm into Toto, and Randy Jackson, now best-known for sitting near Paula Abdul on *American Idol* and saying "dawg" a lot. These are the people Springsteen trusted to convey his music. Dave Marsh maintains longtime fans rejected the *Human Touch* era because he "toured with a black band and a [slightly] blacker beat." In fact, fans abandoned that music—and Springsteen rarely played any of it after the end of his '93 tour—because it represented a rare fall into the slick and generic.

Why are the knives out? Even the Rolling Stones and Bob Dylan were at last allowed to make pretty good records without fans and critics reminding everyone they weren't at the *Sticky Fingers* or *Blonde on Blonde* level anymore. But fans and critics came to those conclusions about the Stones and Dylan after the two had been releasing lousy records for a long time. There was no precedent to *Human Touch*, the first Springsteen album since his '73 debut *Greetings from Asbury Park, N.J.* with genuinely not-good songs on it, performed by a crew of frosty studio musicians who have roughly the same relationship to the E Street Band as the cast of *Beatlemania* had to John, Paul, George, and Ringo. Instead of using the new players as a way to explore something new, he tried to get them to sound like the E Street Band. Throughout *Human Touch*, you hear Springsteen thinking about what he should do, fussing over choices. On all his previous records you heard the product of his thinking, here you heard him thinking. He wanted listeners to know he was happy. Fine. As with the tortured Van Morrison, who wouldn't want Springsteen and his characters to enjoy some happiness? The problem was that this happiness was not documented in an interesting way.

Part of the problem was the length of the record. Fifty-nine minutes long, probably because Springsteen felt he could justify his long absence if he delivered quantity, it makes room for what feels like every half-baked idea he came up with during the time, although when *Tracks* came out fans were stuck with another dozen performances of similar random quality. One other outtake, perversely stuck on the *18 Tracks* sampler, turned out to be more worthy: "Trouble River," which answers the musical question of what would it sound like if the guitar lines of Hank Mizell's "Easy Money" and "We Got the Beat" by the Go-Go's got married and had a baby.

"Human Touch" delivered evidence of what little that worked and plenty that didn't on the album it gave a name. The song didn't really start until the bridge, when the crack of Porcaro's drums snaps everyone to attention—just like Max Weinberg does—again begging the question of what musical reason Springsteen had for playing with new people if he was just going to try to get them to sound like the E Street Band. Springsteen shouted during the instrumental break as if he was trying to get himself excited, and offered up both a wonderful self-deprecating come-on ("I know I ain't nobody's bargain/But hell a little touchup and a little paint") and, if you were lucky enough to have the full album version and not the single, a brief, pungent guitar solo worthy of Richard Thompson.

That was about as good as *Human Touch* got. "Soul Driver" was one of the new songs debuted at the Christic show, vague both lyrically ("Rode through forty nights of the gospels' rain") and musically (Sam Moore was brought in to prop it up). "57 Channels (and Nothin' On)" stood out among the bass-centric compositions, but it was delivered in an overwrought manner: When the narrator shot out the TV set, Springsteen didn't trust the song to do its job without a glass-shattering sound effect. (To be fair, this terse, claustrophobic version was superior to the ill-fitting 12-inch remix supervised by Steve Van Zandt. Come home, Arthur Baker. All is forgiven!) The rockers like "Gloria's Eyes" and the outtakes "Leavin' Train" and "Seven Angels" felt readymade, phoned in from Springsteen's memory of 10,000 songs. Rockers that made the record—"Roll of the Dice," "All or Nothin' at All," and "The Long Goodbye"—were all built on lyrical and musical clichés and carried too much baggage to rock freely. "Real Man" was a polished, empty rocker, with lines like "I got to know if your love is real." When you're quoting your own songs, you're not ready to make a record. "Man's Job" offered a pleasant groove and Jackson's most distinctive bass on the album, but not much more. The elemental "With Every Wish" was closer to the ground but not quite real, listening in on a professional songwriter revisiting

190

his "have mercy on the man who doubts what he's sure of" theme.

It was a shock to hear the truly grounded traditional ballad "Pony Boy" at the end of *Human Touch*: just Springsteen on guitar, he and Scialfa singing (some mild synthesizer and percussion filled in the arrangement in later verses), apparently to a child. After all the Big Statements of the previous 11 performances, "Pony Boy" was a frank, modest lullaby, nothing more, nothing less, an indication of what was important to Springsteen, and it served as a link to the more interesting album about family that he released the same day as *Human Touch*.

Toward the end of the lengthy recording of *Human Touch*, Springsteen wrote "Living Proof," a tough rocker about how family can save even a self-pitying millionaire rock'n'roller. Aside from relying a bit too much on God to make its point, the song manages to speak loudly and deeply without being too sentimental. In its small story it delivers a Big Noise. Springsteen thought at first that "Living Proof" was the song he needed to cap *Human Touch* (as "Dancing in the Dark" accomplished for *Born in the U.S.A.*), but as he quickly wrote and recorded, it was instead the beginning of an entirely new album, *Lucky Town*. Most of the record was recorded at his home studio, with Bittan and others adding coloring elsewhere. Of Springsteen's homemade records, *Lucky Town* was the one that sounded most like it was recorded by a band. It was in many ways the antithesis of *Human Touch*: earthy instead of shiny, spontaneous instead of overrehearsed, terse instead of long-winded, coherent instead of all over the place. So when the two records came out the same day, the shorthand was *Human Touch* bad, *Lucky Town* good. In retrospect, that's way too simple (although even most of those who liked *Human Touch* acknowledged the relative superiority of *Lucky Town*). *Lucky Town* is a stronger set and feels more like a unified album, but it's truly top-notch only when compared to *Human Touch*. Indeed, the one stinker on *Lucky Town*, the gaudy "Leap of Faith," is the one performance that could have fit on the other record.

Most of what keeps *Lucky Town* off the top tier of Springsteen albums is its musical sameness and lack of a great drummer. Van Morrison stalwart Garry Mallaber keeps the drummer's seat warm here, and he's a perfectly good technician—he made *Moondance* swing—but it sounds like his job on *Lucky Town* was to give the click tracks Springsteen recorded to a slightly more live feel. The hard rockers here, namely the title track and "Souls of the Departed," need something more hot-headed pushing them along. The drums are the only polite thing on *Lucky Town* and, hence, its weak link.

From the moment it began, the album's opener, "Better Days," brought with it a jump in energy and directness from *Human Touch*, Springsteen dragging his pick across the strings, his optimism unforced. He probably didn't need all his sisters singing along with him to make his point that things are good, but they didn't take up too much space. There's humor here: in "Lucky Town," the narrator toasted his beloved's good looks—and his good health. In "Local Hero," one of many songs on the two albums that take as a given the singer's fame, the narrator is confronted by his past when he sees a black velvet painting of himself hanging in the window of a store. Springsteen presents it in the right self-deflating tone from someone whose songs sometimes are as much about the songwriter's mythology as the topic at hand. "Lucky Town" breaks down the barrier between songwriter and narrator: Even if it is not personally autobiographical, it feels that way. The same impulse drives the lovely "Book of Dreams," in which the narrator is back to the scene of "Walk Like a Man" (I'll refrain from buying into the Springsteen mythology that it's the same man drifting from song to song), except now all he can wonder over is his bride.

You can hear Springsteen work through what it means to write about relationships in "Souls of the Departed," the angriest song on *Lucky Town*. It careens from an American soldier outside Basra dreaming he sees the souls of Iraqi soldiers rising to a mother in East Compton mourning the schoolyard murder of her son to a man tucking in his son: "All I can think of is what if it would've been him instead/I want to build me a wall so high nothing can burn it down." Well, he can build a wall so high nothing can burn it down. Springsteen, as narrator or real person, is protected from the world he can't get out of his head, and for now all he can do is cough up a bit of earned self-loathing (as opposed to the gratuitous variety). The thick accompaniment, all but Mallaber's drums performed by Springsteen, ratchets up the anger and turns ominous, but there's something preventing the song from reaching a fever pitch.

I found out what it was missing one afternoon in September '03, on the tail end of the *Rising* tour, while Springsteen and the E Street Band were conducting a sound check at a stadium in Hartford, Connecticut. Springsteen called for "Souls of the Departed," a song the E Street Band had never played publicly until then. (They would open the evening's performance with the song.) They ran through it well. It was as if they had just heard the studio version and they replicated it. Over the next 25 minutes, they played it four more times. Each time it got dirtier, angrier. Linear guitar lines turn into stuttered, spat-out exclamations, snare drums and floor toms rattled with the violence of the lyric. What was missing on the album version? More than anything else, the song was screaming for Nils Lofgren's guitar and Max Weinberg's drums. It needed the E Street Band.

The happiness on *Lucky Town* is earned and equivocal, which differentiates it from the generic expressions of delight on *Human Touch*. At the end of the record awaits "My Beautiful Reward," in which a man looking back at his life turns into a bird or imagines he turns into a bird, soars over this world en route to the next destination, at the edge between the worlds, still searching, like the narrator on "The Rising" who dies "like a catfish dancin' on the end of my line." He's satisfied in a way, but still searching. You don't have to believe in any afterlife to find that moving. It ended a record that, unlike *Human Touch*, was a genuinely interesting, thoughtful, and provocative deliberation on happiness, one with as many questions as answers.

It was disorienting listening to *Human Touch* and *Lucky Town*, arriving as they did the same day. The former built up an arbitrary artifice; the latter was a serious attempt to burn down that wall. When Springsteen announced he would tour behind the records, one wondered which album would hold sway. Springsteen realized it had been a long time since he had a hit record and he needed to do some more publicity than usual, so he agreed to his first live television performance, on *Saturday Night Live*, with Tom Hanks hosting. He brought with him a core band of Bittan on keyboards, and journeymen Shane Fontayne on guitar, Tommy Sims on bass, and Zach Alford on drums. All had plenty of experience as session men and on *SNL* they performed sturdy, close-to-the-ground music. It was as if Springsteen sought to front his own personal Crazy Horse. The results weren't outstanding and you could see and hear that this was not a band with a 20-year history, but it was a reasonable start. For those who were worried, *Lucky Town* won out.

Not for long. Rather than see the *SNL* gig as a limited success worth building on, Springsteen apparently decided it was insufficient and hired six more singers (one of whom played guitar) for a slick arena tour, a pointless outing fossilized in the live *MTV* ~~Unplugged~~. The performance is bombastic and clunky, with no subtlety, ruining perfectly good song after perfectly good song, making the listener beg for at least Porcaro and Jackson. Springsteen sounds lost. He's distanced from the band, which has no believable interaction with him, and his singing is tired. Particular derision should be directed toward the version of "Light of Day," which manages to make a terrific performance piece bland. If Columbia ever needs to make extra-nice to Springsteen, it should offer to take this off the market. They can deny it ever existed. Few will want to argue.

The tour did get better in its second half, as the set list turned a bit more elastic and Springsteen began opening the show with a brief solo set that included unexpected songs like the gospel standard "Satan's Jewel Crown." Special guests like Southside Johnny and Joe Ely enlivened some shows, but one night at Madison Square Garden the crowd was so mean to Terence Trent D'Arby that Springsteen all but went medieval on the audience's collective ass. Most of the shows on the '92–'93 tour were about nothing other than a pro doing his job. A jokey sequence in the middle of "Glory Days" at one of the early shows underlined this. During the breakdown, Springsteen talked about looking forward to the long tour before him. "I see adventure. I see financial reward," he said, and then turned to the issue of his not topping the charts with either of his two new albums. "I see those albums going back up the charts. I see them rising past that old Def Leppard, past that Kris Kross. I see them all the way up past 'Weird' Al Yankovic, even." He riffed a bit, then returned to reality. "Wait a minute, we're slipping down the charts. We're going down, down, out of sight, into the darkness." This was, apparently, what he was thinking about.

The gambit was not doomed. Especially with a catalogue as deep and malleable as Springsteen and at least one new album of good material, there was nothing necessarily wrong with touring alongside unfamiliar players. Artists have to shake things up on occasion and do more than simply switch where the same old people are standing. But it's a fool's errand to take a bunch of second-tier talents, ask 'em to pretend to be E Streeters, and expect to perform anything new or worthwhile. Springsteen couldn't have taken to the road solo; he wanted to fill arenas. But he should have gone on the road with a band that did not try to sound like the E Street Band, a band that could have developed its own identity. In '86, Elvis Costello released two records with two bands and went on the road with both of them; there was an almost limitless number of possibilities. But Springsteen decided to try to replicate the past with new faces, something that rarely works in life or art.

There's a deeper question: Should Springsteen have released *Human Touch* at all? On some level he knew it wasn't good enough, because he wouldn't release it alone. If all he'd emerged with after five years away was the low-key *Lucky Town*, written and recorded in roughly a month, maybe he felt people would wonder too much why it took so long. *Human Touch* was a creative exercise without which he never would have gotten to *Lucky Town*. It was an experiment, which is what artists should undertake, but it was an experiment that failed, which artists shouldn't release. *Human Touch* is a document of what an artist needed to go through to regain his footing, but doesn't come close to Springsteen's previous standards for what made a releasable studio album.

Springsteen released one new song in '94, "Streets of Philadelphia," written at the request of Jonathan Demme, who was looking for a theme song for a film he was directing, *Philadelphia*. It was a movie about AIDS and Springsteen has acknowledged that Demme looked to him, a rocker with a very straight image, to provide music that was safe for a hetero—or more important, latently homophobic—audience. That's also partly why the film starred two safe actors, Tom Hanks and Denzel Washington, and the other big-name artist on the sound track was Neil Young. The song "Streets of Philadelphia" was superb, sounding modern yet rooted in Springsteen's longtime interests, but it started a pattern of Springsteen needing an external reason to take a new song public—or even create a song worth releasing. Demme's movie needed a song (and after "Streets of Philadelphia" became an Oscar-winning hit, other directors called), *Greatest Hits* needed some new blood, the reunion tour needed a closing statement, 9/11 necessitated the *Rising* songs. Many of the songs were top-notch, but they do not appear to have arisen organically so much as work for hire.

A song as moving and dead-on as "Streets of Philadelphia" doesn't need to justify itself. Springsteen has often talked of being a lonely misfit as a teenager, and lines like "I was unrecognizable to myself" make sense in an AIDS context but are also of a piece with so much else he's written. And the line "receive me brother with your faithless kiss," half-buried in the last verse, the sound of a dying man too spent to summon up his anger, adds a level of complexity missing in all the "That's What Friends Are For" bromides. The song fills a large canvas. It's not only about AIDS any more than Tony Kushner's ambitious *Angels in America* was only about AIDS. (Part of promoting "Streets of Philadelphia" included submitting to an interview in *The Advocate*, a required stop for celebrities looking to establish or solidify credibility in the gay press, featuring hilarious softball questions like "So you actually met gay people?")

There was no new Springsteen album on which to place "Streets of Philadelphia." A solo project in '94 was aborted in favor of a *Greatest Hits* collection that came out in February '95. As such sets go, it wasn't bad. Despite pretending that Springsteen's career began after he started releasing hit singles (neither *Greetings from Asbury Park, N.J.* nor *The Wild, the Innocent, and the E Street Shuffle* was represented), it captured 13 of the obvious highlights, brought in "Streets of Philadelphia," and included four previously unreleased performances with the E Street Band, including three newly recorded ones. Alas, for space reasons, Springsteen included the shorter single version of "Human Touch," extracting the guitar solo, one of the few lively moments on that album.

This brief E Street Band reunion was born of commercial considerations, not artistic ones, and it was supposed to be the beginning of something more lasting. In a feature for the *New York Times*, Neil Strauss reported that Springsteen "wants to finish recording a solo album in the next few weeks and record an album with the band this summer." That next studio album with the E Street Band wouldn't appear for another seven summers, '02 rather than '95.

The point of *Greatest Hits*, aside from a nice injection into everyone's bank accounts, was to keep Springsteen in the news. Three years after the *Human Touch/Lucky Town* release, the new tracks were there to convince the audience that Springsteen was a performer still releasing worthwhile new material. The commercial part worked: *Greatest Hits* was Springsteen's first Number One since *Tunnel of Love*, more for the catalogue material than the newer contributions. "Secret Garden" was a minor hit, although it enjoyed a second life two years later when used in the film *Jerry McGuire*.

The idea behind the new tracks may have been to get people thinking of Springsteen in the present tense, but two of the four "new" songs were in fact oldies, songs written and recorded for *Born in the U.S.A.* "Murder Incorporated" was a remixed version of the original '92 studio session, while "This Hard Land" was an adequate redo of another song from that period (the sharper '83 version wound up on *Tracks*). The two genuinely "new" songs on the album suggested he did have something new to say with the E Street Band if he wanted to—even if the topic of one of the songs was whether he had anything to say to them. Both of them were sweet-sounding ballads with plenty of uncertainty lurking underneath. "Secret Garden" was cut from the same musical cloth as "Streets of Philadelphia." It was a tribute to the unknowability of women, all sorts of confusion at war with the devotional tone, taken on at the end by a persuasive nudge of a sax solo from Clemons.

Even more complicated was "Blood Brothers," which was tried several ways during the *Greatest Hits* sessions. There's an overtly rocking version featuring a guitar line borrowed from the Bobby Fuller Four that would show up again in *The Rising*'s "Further Up on the Road." Released on a bonus EP around the same time as *Greatest Hits*, the fast "Blood Brothers" moved efficiently but didn't end up satisfying, most likely because writer and band were still feeling their way around the song, trying to re-create an E Street feel rather than figuring out what the song needed, although that might be a logical approach on a record and a song about looking back. The version that did make the record was softer, more deliberate, almost overheard in tone. As a writer Springsteen is well known for final verses that wrap up emotions if not stories ("This Hard Land" and "Reason to Believe" are prime pieces of evidence), but "Blood Brothers," a song about reconnecting, included one of the few sturdy ambivalent last verses of his career, peaking with "I don't even know why, I don't know why I made the call/Or if any of this matters anymore." Springsteen's post–*Born in the U.S.A.* albums all examined the complexity of romantic love; the strength of "Blood Brothers" comes from its illuminating how love for your friends can be complex too.

Springsteen being a man who wants to project a positive public image and the E Street Band mythology being such an important part of his public image, this ambivalence wouldn't last long. On the final night of both the '99–'00 and '02–'03 tours with the E Street Band, Springsteen closed the show with the otherwise-never-performed "Blood Brothers," with a new final verse that replaced the ambivalence of the original with unambiguous love for his bandmates.

What I am about to describe may seem corny but was quite moving. As he sang that replacement final verse, Springsteen stood at his center microphone, each hand stretched out and grasping that of a band member. Except for Weinberg, Federici, and Bittan, tethered to their drums or keyboards, all the members of the E Street Band stood across the front of the stage, holding hands. It was an ideal overlap of content and form. There's a bit of exaggeration here ("battles won and lost"?) but those in the audience saw and heard a man expressing his love for and commitment to his most sympathetic accompanists. Since there was no guarantee at the end of either tour that the band would ever again play together, it felt like a punctuation mark at the end of a long shared career. Both times, at Madison Square Garden (last show in '00) and Shea Stadium (last show in '03), some members of the band were visibly crying. A cynic might argue that the E Street mythology is so thick that even the band members hang on to it; others would wonder whether some part of the myth has become true. The device will get tired if they tour half a dozen more times and end each tour with the same song of affirmation, but for now it's a vivid reminder of why the band matters so much to so many people, what fans project onto them and expect of them.

That altered last verse was far away from anyone's mind in the early weeks on '95, and Springsteen soon found himself back in the studio at his California home, working on a solo project. He had written "The Ghost of Tom Joad" for the E Street reunion sessions, but now he hushed the number and recorded it with a small, unobtrusive band that included Gary Tallent on bass, Danny Federici on keyboard, and Garry Mallaber on drums. Their job was simple: Don't get in the way. The sound is as quiet and stripped-down as a full band can be, in large part because the almost-whispered lyrics are so direct, so plainspoken, that even a slight amount of ornamentation would pretty the song up and distract from the thick emotions in the lyric and the singing.

The title track of *The Ghost of Tom Joad*, released late in '95, introduced the album and stated its concerns. The elaborate, wordy lyric-writing style of *Human Touch* and *Lucky Town* was gone. (Even on the better songs on *Lucky Town*, like "Living Proof," it took Springsteen a 26-word run-on sentence to say "my child is crying.") Everything was pared down, as you might expect of a work inspired by the title character of John Steinbeck's *The Grapes of Wrath*, that epic tale of American dreams lost and found by Okies escaping the Dust Bowl for illusory work in California. Springsteen has said since *Darkness on the Edge of Town* (whose "Adam Raised a Cain" bore a resemblance to Steinbeck's *East of Eden*) that he was attracted to Steinbeck's characters and stories, but he was a follower of Steinbeck's method, too. *Working Days*, a collection of the journal entries Steinbeck penned when he was writing *The Grapes of Wrath*, finds the author pursued by the demons of self-doubt, self-loathing, and perhaps some

bona fide paranoia. Even more than the novel, Springsteen was inspired by the film version of *The Grapes of
Wrath*, starring Henry Fonda and directed by John
Ford. The film veered between the theatrical-stagey and
the realistic, and Nunnally Johnson's screenplay sought
to create complex, believable Okie characters, but
shared with Steinbeck's novel a failure to consider the
bad guys in California as anything other than card-
board villains. On *The Ghost of Tom Joad*, Springsteen
went his inspirations one better by humanizing those on
both sides of the line: The border-patrol guards in "The
Line" were as tragically human as the poor people they
hunted down, and even the angry racist in "Galveston
Bay" could perform an act of relative grace.

Underlying *The Ghost of Tom Joad* was Springsteen's belief that California in the nineties had much in
common with the California of the thirties, but this
time migrant workers and those desperate to escape
north from Mexico were the new Okies, brought up as
mules, forced to hustle on street corners and cook
methamphetamine to get by. By the end of *The Grapes
of Wrath*, Tom Joad was radicalized and moved to act,
but he was luckier than the characters on Springsteen's
record, who, for the most part, were too desperate stay-
ing alive or moving to arrive at such epiphanies.

Note that all I'm writing about are the words. *The
Ghost of Tom Joad* is as accomplished lyrically as any
record you can name, but it's musically quite samey and
will likely suffer the fate of being one of those records

everyone agrees is terrific, but no one actually listens to its dark tales for more than a song or two at a time. Quiet but angry, the record is full of songs in which poignant portraits and brilliant observations are conveyed by a narrator too stunned to raise his voice. Word for word, it's more precise and provocative than *Nebraska*, its clearest antecedent among Springsteen albums, but it offers no musical diversity.

It does a disservice to these songs to extract individual lines from their fully realized whole selves, but there are individual lines that speak volumes, like "seems you can't get any more than half-free" from the ex-con trying to walk the line in "Straight Time" or "My hand slipped up her skirt, everything slipped my mind" by the shoe-salesman-turned-killer in "Highway 29," one of many songs that have a hazy, smoky, dream-like quality. In "Youngstown," later claimed in "Atlantic City" style by the reunited E Street Band, the singer sees "smokestacks reachin' like the arms of God." The choices these characters face are intolerable: in "Sinaloa Cowboys" two brothers cross to the north and wind up cooking methamphetamine because "You could spend a year in the orchards/Or make half as much in one ten-hour shift"; one dies in an explosion, the other digs up the 10 grand they'd saved to bury him. Best of all might have been "The Line," about a man very much like the narrator of *Nebraska*'s "Highway Patrolman" (maybe this is Joe Roberts's new job after he finally got fired for letting his brother get away all the time), who falls for

Louisa, a woman trying to cross with her young child. He brings her across, confronts his friend and colleague to do so, and loses her forever. Like a character from a dark fairy tale, all he does now is search for her. Like most of the characters here, he'll never find anything. "Galveston Bay" is the most optimistic song on the record, even if it's stuffed with death and a cameo from members of the Texas Klan. It begins and ends with different men, ostensibly on opposing sides, kissing sleeping family members and looking out at the same body of water. The idea is we're all connected, like it or not, although Springsteen is too hardheaded to have them throw down their arms and sing "Kumbaya" together. The album ends with "My Best Was Never Good Enough," a list of intentional clichés delivered bitterly. As "Reason to Believe" did on *Nebraska*, "My Best Was Never Good Enough" concludes *The Ghost of Tom Joad* with a singer convinced that life is nothing more than a bad joke.

This wasn't fist-pumping music by a long shot, so when Springsteen decided to promote the album with his first full-length solo tour, it led to some of the most dour performances of his career. The first leg of the jaunt could have been called the "Take Your Medicine Tour," all sad songs and angry songs, with only fleeting moments of release. After Springsteen got more comfortable playing with the songs and guiding his audience, he realized he wouldn't ruin the *Tom Joad* songs by adding some more liberating material. The second leg was much more balanced: gloomy *Nebraska* and *Tom Joad* numbers complemented by a wider variety of compositions, like "Red Headed Woman," and a new (and still unreleased) song called "Pilgrim in the Temple of Love" that anticipated much of the plot of *Bad Santa*. Of the unreleased material he debuted, "The Hitter" and "Brothers Under the Bridge" were unrelieved downers, and "Long Time Comin'" made impending parenthood sound like time for regret and promises. But "It's the Little Things That Count" and "Sell It and They Will Come" were sly, low-key, and funny. It was good to hear Springsteen still indulging that side.

Although the tour eventually loosened up, when it was over Springsteen went back and started writing and recording another album in the *Tom Joad* vein. It appeared as if he wanted to be Pete Seeger when he grew up. But, as with so many of Springsteen's recording projects, he set it aside (he returned to some of this material for *Devils & Dust* in '05) and considered other opportunities. Just as he did in late '94 when another solo project stalled, he looked backward and turned his attention to compiling a four-CD collection of unreleased material, *Tracks*. Much of the music on *Tracks* was wonderful (no need to dissect it again here; I've been citing individual tracks in context), but it was released at roughly the same time as a coffee-table book of lyrics, *Songs*, in which Springsteen (with the help of Robert Santelli) wrote brief essays at the beginning of each album's lyrics, explaining what he was trying to do on each disc. Eager for publicity, Springsteen submitted to many extended interviews supporting the box set and the book, but it was all too much. It's the music that's supposed to do the talking, not the performer. But Springsteen wanted to control the discussion, so he made sure his opinion on what his songs and records meant would hold sway by repeating them over and over and over. As Ricky Ricardo might demand, "Stop 'splainin'."

On *Tracks* you can listen to the music and not have to read the interviews; *Songs* forced you to submit to Springsteen's interpretations of his own material. (The explaining continued at two quixotic solo benefits for *DoubleTake* magazine in Somerville, Massachusetts, during a break in the *Rising* tour, at which he took adulatory questions from the audience.) Like so many other aging rockers, Springsteen was now in the business of explaining himself. His brief essays in *Songs* flattened his songs, insisting fans could think of them in only one way. Critics of a songwriter's work have to do their work at some level of abstraction. Springsteen is the only person who can write about this material with authoritative credibility, but his notes in *Songs* often veer toward empty rock-critic abstractions. "*Born to Run* was the dividing line." "The precision of the story-telling in these types of songs is very important." Arrogance popped up, too: "Our band was built well over many years, for difficult times." It was like when *The Rising* came out and someone decided that it would be promoted as The Official Album of Sept. 11™, and Springsteen would tell anyone within earshot about the guy who shouted at him in a parking lot shortly after the attacks, "Hey Bruce! We need ya!" The problem with being called the savior of rock'n'roll for almost your entire adult life is that eventually you believe it, at least partly.

The savior of rock'n'roll has to actually play some rock'n'roll every now and then to keep the title, so the release of *Tracks*, coupled with Springsteen's induction into the Rock and Roll Hall of Fame, made a more permanent reconstitution of the E Street Band inevitable. Springsteen was inducted in a loving and funny manner by U2's Bono (who sang a snatch of "Sandy" during his speech), and Springsteen ended his (inevitably) lengthy acceptance speech by citing the members of the E Street Band, with whom he had not spent more than a week in the studio in 15 years. He spoke of them one by one and saved his kindest words for Clarence Clemons, a man absent from Springsteen's music for many years but clearly on The Boss's mind: "Clarence has been a source of myth and light and enormous strength for me on stage. He has filled my heart so many nights and I love it when he wraps me in those arms at the end of the night. The night we first stood together, I looked over at C and it looked like his head reached into the clouds. And I felt like a mere mortal scurrying upon the earth, you know. But he always lifted me up. Way, way, way up. Together we told a story of the possibilities of friendship, a story older than the ones that I was writing and a story I could never have told without him at my side." It was time to bring Clemons back to his side and discover whether their shared story held any more possibilities.

Chapter 7

Nils Lofgren, Steve Van Zandt, and the Last Secret of Rock'n'Roll

With the possible exception of the Animals, who roared back to life in '77 with *Before We Were So Rudely Interrupted*, there has never been a rock'n'roll band whose reunion work equaled that which they did before their breakup. (Not that the high quality did Eric Burdon and Co. any favors in the marketplace. The reunion album was not a big hit.) The work can be quite good, or it can stink like the "new" tracks that soured the Beatles' *Anthology* series. But, except for the Animals' thunderous exception, there's been no band to emerge from a lengthy layoff unscathed. Even pretty good bands who were on the rocks for short periods of time, like Squeeze, returned diminished. A band is an organic thing, like a flower, and if you don't water it for a long time, you're not going to be happy with the results when you start up again.

That's the history Bruce Springsteen and the E Street Band faced in '02 when they entered Southern Tracks Recording in Atlanta to work with producer Brendan O'Brien. The band had played well, sometimes far beyond well, on an extended reunion tour, but a brief attempt at recording some new songs in New York after the tour ended left Springsteen cool. The relative failure of those New York sessions led Springsteen to realize it was time to try something really new with the band in the studio. On the advice of Sony Records president Don Ienner, Springsteen met with Brendan O'Brien, a Georgia-based producer who had helmed popular records for Pearl Jam and Rage Against the Machine as well as a pair of terrific shoulda-been-monster-hit records by his sometime bandmate Dan Baird. Springsteen and O'Brien clicked. Leaving behind his longtime and by now overly chummy regular production team, Springsteen brought the band to Atlanta and tried out a new sound. It was more "produced" than any previous E Street Band record: You don't hear the band as a band. Indeed, the band sounds more like unusually intuitive session musicians. O'Brien's sound gives each player a separate space and the sound is too clean. After the hard-edged three-guitar attack of the reunion tour, it was a surprise to hear Springsteen and the band return to the studio and end up with an album on which the lead instrument was often a violin, performed by longtime collaborator and new E Streeter Soozie Tyrell. The E Street Band reformed to make a very good record, a record that was very much of its cultural and political moment, but it didn't deliver a beginning-to-end great record that could stand with its seventies and eighties classics. Some individual songs were monumental, such as the almost unbearable "You're Missing," its details of loss so precise and the performance so emotional, it's one of those songs, like Lucinda Williams's "Sweet Old World" or Bob Dylan's "Every Grain of Sand" that is so true, so beautiful, so deep that it's hard to listen to it clearly, impossible to listen to it dispassionately.

Across *The Rising*, there was enough first-rate material to fill a superlative but much shorter, quieter, and coherent record: "Lonesome Day," "Into the Fire," "Nothing Man," "Empty Sky," "You're Missing," "The Rising," "Paradise," "My City of Ruins." (Hey, *Born to Run* had only eight songs and few listeners found that incomplete.) But Springsteen's insistence, for once, to put out almost everything he finished during the sessions (15 of 17 songs made the cut) meant that songs that were filler or simply didn't work conceptually got on board, too. While *Tracks* showed how ruthless Springsteen could be, exiling top-rank songs and performances because they didn't fit in with a specific concept, *The Rising* showed that even he could leave in too much, because almost every song included at least one stirring moment, like the generic rocker "Countin' on a Miracle," which delivered merely the expected but sported one of the great majestic bridges of the E Street Band's

215

career, or "The Fuse," which meandered behind a busy arrangement but started with an exciting mix of beat box and guitar fuzz. Happy to be back in the studio with the E Street Band, Springsteen wanted to let all of it out.

Still, this was a record with him in the forefront: On the deluxe-packaging version of *The Rising* there are precisely 99 photographs of Springsteen, two of Danny Federici, and one of each of the other members of the E Street Band. On record, he was still holding everything close. It was only when he started playing these songs live that Springsteen truly showed why he's at his best with the E Street Band.

The biggest difference between the reunion and *Rising* tours—and the crucial difference that made the latter superior to the former—is that the reunion tour was all about looking back at former triumphs while the *Rising* tour took a deep breath and then peered forward. "There used to be this thing called a rock'n'roll show," was the message of the reunion tour. "We know there's no such thing anymore, but we used to do it better than anyone else. We're still pretty great. Anyway, this is what we used to do." Rock'n'roll as a cultural moment had passed by the time the E Street Band returned to the road, reduced to classic songs reconfigured in our minds as half-remembered car commercials and context-free ditties for our young children to warble. The rock'n'roll era ended some time between the release of Neil Young and Crazy Horse's *Ragged Glory* and the death of Kurt Cobain, roughly around the time "hot topic" changed from something exciting to talk about to the name of a retail chain in shopping malls that specialized in goth and metal fashion. When someone in purple hair, covered with tattoos and sporting a safety-pin-pierced cheek smiles at you in a Hot Topic store and asks, "How may I help you, sir?", the co-option of rock'n'roll culture by commercial culture is pretty much complete. The good guys lost. Think about it the next time you see Bob Dylan on TV selling underpants. In this context, where a song like Dylan's "Love Sick" is permanently reduced from ragged meditation to slick marketing collateral, the E Street Band's reunion tour was about reminding people about life before bands starting boasting to one another about who scored the more lucrative corporate-sponsorship deal.

I don't want to simplify and make it seem like the reunion tour was only about nostalgia and the *Rising* tour was only about the excitement of the present tense and the promise of the future. Some of the new songs from *The Rising* never did connect live, particularly "The Fuse" and "Countin' on a Miracle," which the band played most nights the first half of the tour, and the every-night "Mary's Place," which sounded more inferior to its antecedents "Rosalita" and "Thundercrack" every night. Casting "Mary's Place," a party song, as a tale of how someone left behind on 9/11 (thinking about "that black hole on the horizon") uses music and community (not to mention references to "Heat Wave" and at least three early-seventies Van Morrison songs) to help him feel better makes the song sag under the weight. The band performs energetic enough versions of "Mary's Place," but maybe the reason it fails live is that the performance was about Springsteen's needs, not his audience's. The clue for that comes from the key verse in the song, after a breakdown, as the band gradually draws power and comes back in.

As Springsteen repeats "Waitin' for that shout from the crowd" to the arena and stadium crowds, he doesn't have to wait. He receives it, over and over. There's a sense in his public statements that Springsteen wrote and recorded *The Rising* to perform a sort of public service, to capture the awful feelings of September '01 and help make sense of them for/with his audience. But when he performed "Mary's Place," it felt like Springsteen wrote that song for *The Rising* and played it every night because it made *him* feel better. Perhaps songs like "Mary's Place" don't work because Springsteen has abandoned humor in the studio. Bruce has two voices fighting in his head: the serious voice and the silly one. On record at least, the serious voice has prevailed by a knockout. Not since *The River*, 24 years old as I write this paragraph, with "Sherry Darling," "Out in the Street," "You Can Look (But You Better Not Touch)," "Cadillac Ranch," "Crush on You," "I'm a Rocker," and "Ramrod," has Springsteen produced a new studio record that offers a healthy chunk of fun. (No, votes for "Glory Days" will not be counted. No one, except perhaps

America's Dumbest Rock Critic George Will, thinks there's sustained joy anywhere on *Born in the U.S.A.*)

Whatever you might think of individual songs and how they played out before a crowd, at least *Rising* audiences had the pleasure of witnessing a band trying to work out something new. Most of the main set derived from the new record at a time when the Who, a typical example, were on their umpteenth farewell/reunion/anniversary tour, having not even tried to record a new cut since the early eighties. (Down to a limping duo, Townshend and Daltrey eventually bit the bullet and recorded a pair of new tunes in '03. You don't want to know.) And one *Rising* song that fell flat on the new record, "Waitin' on a Sunny Day," turned out to be a live standout, a sober but endlessly enjoyable counter to the ravages of "Empty Sky" and "You're Missing." (Most nights, the band played the smiling "Waitin' on a Sunny Day" after that particularly somber and quiet one-two punch.) Strangely, "Into the Fire," one of the subtle standouts on *The Rising*, quickly emerged as a set-deflating clunker live, thanks to a bombastic vocal introduction and a heavy arrangement that simply stopped cold just as the coda on the record felt about to lift off, particularly deadening to a song that closed the main set most nights. The E Street Band has a rich history of taking songs to new levels just as the recorded version comes to an end—"Racing in the Street," "Prove It All Night," and "Out in the Street" serve as thrilling evidence—but onstage "Into the Fire" was too clipped to fly.

The reunion tour had an infinitely superior peak set-ender—the hard-rocking, hilarious "Light of Day"—but the reunion tour as a whole didn't peak until its very end, during a 10-night stay at Madison Square Garden, because it wasn't until then, more than 100 shows into the tour, that they finally got around to playing new songs, the thing that keeps a band vital. Sure, warhorses like "Born to Run" and "Prove It All Night" still sounded great after all these years, but what did that prove other than the band members had kept up their chops and their communications skills? So they still had it. Who with ears was arguing to the contrary?

Until the very end of the tour, the only new song played to audiences on the reunion go-round was "Land of Hope and Dreams," which debuted as the last encore song the first night of the tour and held that spot most nights thereafter. Springsteen and the band couldn't hope for a better song to go out on. A piercing hard-rock guitar intro gives way to gospel keyboard and vocal lines, Clarence Clemons's only great post–*Born in the U.S.A.* sax solo, the most dramatic drum fills of Max Weinberg's dramatic career, and a mandolin thrown in just to see if the song can take it. There's a reason they played it almost every night since debuting it. The song ranks among the greatest of all Springsteen compositions, a not-too-neat summation of the lyrical and musical themes he's explored for most of his career.

It may have been a song about death—the train in "Land of Hope and Dreams" is headed toward some heaven, the ultimate end of the road—but it's among the most redemptive and optimistic stops in a journey that has sought out many similar stopovers. Springsteen may have been able to maintain his fan base at such a high level for so long because, with few exceptions, his musical impulses have been essentially conservative (especially with the E Street Band, his surprises emerge from within a self-constrained context), but "Land of Hope and Dreams" showed how much new he and the band could squeeze into their usual framework.

That's right: The one new song they played at the end of the Oldies Show was one of their best ever. After three hours of looking back, "Land of Hope and Dreams" showed that the future of Springsteen songs and E Street band performances could be outstanding. With such a shining example of what might be held in store, it would be hard for longtime fans—and let's face it, in '00 pretty much the only fans Springsteen had were longtime fans—to accept the backward-looking show without a grunt of frustration that the band was being too conservative, that they were wallowing in the past when the future looked pretty damn bright.

The music of "Land of Hope and Dreams" is as widescreen and hopeful as the lyrics—"big wheels roll through fields where sunlight streams" and "tomorrow there'll be sunshine/and all this darkness past." And let us now praise Max Weinberg's two brief, perfect drum breaks toward the end. Weinberg stands among the top pop-music drummers ever, up there with Benny Benjamin, Al Jackson, Keith Moon, Charlie Watts, but how many times has Weinberg ever gotten to cut loose? Since joining the band in '74, Weinberg never played a drum solo with the E Street Band. Especially after *The River*, his restraint became his trademark. His short breaks here are melodic and dramatic, forceful yet restrained: it's a drum break, not a drum solo. They mirror the band's first song most nights on the reunion tour, "My Love Will Not Let You Down." Weinberg begins and ends the evening with his wildest and most dramatic moves.

Even when his drums are all you hear, Weinberg is essentially a modest player, making certain he's supporting the song, not getting out in front of it. And then the band comes back in, Springsteen moving into gospel-frontman mode to bring the song and the show to a close. He calls on the crowd to "raise your hands" and it's the one time in the show when he adopts a gospel framework that he's doing it without any humor or irony. He's serious. Springsteen may not believe he can heal his audience through his art, but on songs like this it's clear he thinks his job is to try to make people feel more human, feel more alive, feel more understood. That's a ridiculous amount of stuff to expect of a rock-'n'roll song, but that's what "Land of Hope and Dreams" and maybe only a handful of other songs in all of rock'n'roll deliver. If you're only going to play one new song a night, it doesn't get much better.

"Land of Hope and Dreams" was the pick, of course, but there was more revealed at tour's end. The band debuted two songs in Atlanta just before starting the Madison Square Garden stand—"Further on Up the Road" and "American Skin (41 Shots)"—and another pair, both songwriting collaborations with Joe Grushecky, during the New York shows—"Code of Silence" and "Another Thin Line." Taken separately, the four are strong individual offerings. As a whole, with their shared emphasis on different kinds of community and hope, they feel like the core of the next album that never came out (only one, "Further on Up the Road," appeared on *The Rising* when it was released two years later), just as "The Ties That Bind," "Sherry Darling," "Independence Day," "Point Blank," and "Ramrod," all debuted on the *Darkness on the Edge of Town* tour, became central to Springsteen's next album, *The River*.

"American Skin (41 Shots)" got the most attention. Based on the fate of Amadou Diallo, an unarmed 22-year-old Guinean immigrant shot 41 times by New York City policemen who mistook his wallet for a gun, Springsteen's song is remarkably evenhanded about a defenseless murder, calmly but emotionally looking at the tragedy from all sides (including that of a policeman "kneeling over his body in the vestibule/praying for his life"). In this song, everyone is a victim. Diallo is a victim because he's black, the policemen are victims because the world is a mess. With customary subtlety, the New York City Patrolman's Benevolent Association responded to this fair-minded song by calling for a boycott of Springsteen's Madison Square Garden shows. (Memories last: When Springsteen played the song at a Shea Stadium show three years later, his police escort after the concert evaporated.)

At Madison Square Garden, while the PBA attacks were going on both inside and outside the arena (it was the only time I'd ever heard Springsteen booed), "American Skin (41 Shots)" started with the band's backing vocalists each singing the words "41 shots" one at a time across the stage, first Clemons, then Lofgren, then Van Zandt, then Scialfa. In the middle of the media hurricane, it felt like a gathering of support and strength around Bruce for saying what he was saying (that vocal intro wasn't there in Atlanta): a lovely moment, both unifying and confrontational. As Springsteen sings the ballad, the tension in his singing and the band's arrangement builds, until after the second chorus when the music breaks open and the band plays hard and deep. The tale of the useless death and how it exemplifies American life gets so bad that words cannot express it and only Springsteen's guitar can deliver the cry of love that can get the message across. But after that solo he can say it in words: We're "baptized in each other's blood," irrevocably connected, doomed to relive this

224

tragedy. The song goes out on Clemons's ghostly saxophone, with everything said and nothing resolved.

"Code of Silence" had more modest aspirations, but in its way met its goals. Springsteen's songs written in the nineties with Joe Grushecky never got much of a hearing, mostly because they were on Joe Grushecky records. It's a hard-rocking song about a longtime relationship with "a list of grievances/a hundred miles long," but what song title could have been more provocative at a time when it felt like the PBA wanted to string him up?

Those songs were just for those lucky enough to witness the end of the tour. Fans could hear them, though. "American Skin (41 Shots)" was a popular Napster download within 24 hours of its Atlanta airing and wound up on *Live in New York City*; "Code of Silence" emerged on the bonus CD bundled with the *Essential* compilation; "Another Thin Line" was performed a few times at the end of the *Rising* tour but awaits official release. For the 90 percent of the audience who saw the tour before its very end, there were still fascinating sets, most of the performances retracing old steps, some of them finding new paths to the old wellspring. In particular, "Murder Incorporated" and "Youngstown" felt fresh. The lyrics of "Murder Incorporated," a *Born in the U.S.A.* outtake that gave longtime fans a reason to buy the '95 *Greatest Hits*, are not about much of anything coherent, but their wariness is expressed with maximum conviction. "Youngstown" appeared in acoustic form on *The Ghost of Tom Joad*; here it gets the "Atlantic City" treatment with a howling vocal and a blockbuster Nils Lofgren solo. If you give a guitarist of Lofgren's facility one solo to play almost every night for a year and a half, he's going to think hard about it. As the tour progressed, the solo became more likely to destroy all in its path. Pushed by Weinberg's snare and Federici's evil carnival organ, the song ends in a hail of feedback.

One other rethink of a song, from one of Springsteen's least-regarded albums, provided the reunion tour's most telling moment. During the tour behind *Tom Joad*, during which Springsteen played a quieter but no less furious "Youngstown," he gave an interview to *The New York Times Magazine* that yielded a typically hagiographic profile. He told Nicholas Dawidoff that the best part of touring solo was that he no longer had to "play" himself onstage; now he could "be" himself. Yet there he was, fronting the E Street Band again, playing his old E Street Band material, "playing" himself again. He could play the role well and happily: The long breakdowns in "Tenth Avenue Freeze-Out" and "Light of Day" were witty and entertaining. Even the warhorse "Jungleland" felt more alive without the pumping fists. Some more obvious songs didn't make the set list much. "Born in the U.S.A." appeared in acoustic form when it appeared at all (and that solo version didn't break free until Springsteen added overtones that leaned toward eastern Asia as well as the eastern banks of the Mississippi) and "Dancing in the Dark" got played even more rarely, in a wan countryish arrangement that deserves to remain an unreleased collectible.

No, the tour's most provocative moment came from a less expected source. During the final encore of most shows during that foray, Springsteen, alone on guitar, would start up "If I Should Fall Behind," a relatively obscure but compelling cut from *Lucky Town* about— you guessed it—community and responsibility. The song changed slightly during the tour—Springsteen's guitar developed a hint of a countryish lilt by the final leg—but it retained its essential structure. After the first verse, Springsteen would step away from the microphone and, one by one, other members of the band would sing verses. At the end, they all sang together. It was a bit stagey and contrived, but moving nonetheless: It was, after all, a song about sticking together.

What was happening musically in "If I Should Fall Behind" wasn't as important as what was happening emotionally—or what Springsteen wanted to communicate to his audience emotionally through the song. After guitarist Steve Van Zandt sang his verse, fellow six-stringer Lofgren would step up. Every night, as he stepped toward the microphone, Lofgren would rest his arm on Van Zandt's shoulder, as if to comfort him. Little could be more showbizzy, full of more contrived emotion, but even for those who knew it was coming, it was one of the most affecting moments in a three-hour performance that was all about community, consolation, and camaraderie. It was fake, everyone knew it was fake, yet it felt real, night after night.

That's a difficult achievement. Even the E Street Band can't attain it every time they try. Most nights on the *Rising* tour, the second and final encore would start with "My City of Ruins." Springsteen would start the song solo on piano and after the rest of the band joined in, he would step away from the stool and return the piano to rightful owner Roy Bittan. While the band vamped, Springsteen would walk to his center-stage spot, not planting himself there until after he stopped for a moment with each player, standing beside him or her. The last stop was by Clemons's side, and they would sway a bit together, backs to the crowd, and then Springsteen would return to singing the song. I have no idea what Springsteen said to the band members as he worked his way across the stage. He may have complemented them, he may have told them how pleased he was to be playing with them, or he may have said nothing of emotional import. But let's assume he did speak to them about things that matter. It didn't come off that way. It felt like an act. But, as I just asked us to assume, it might not have been an act, but instead something quite real that developed organically. Still, in the end, it didn't matter whether it was real or spontaneous because it didn't feel real or spontaneous. The choreography in "If I Should Fall Behind" looked fake but felt real; the choreography in "My City of Ruins" may well have been as real as anything in life but looked fake.

The best moments on the *Rising* tour were the ones that couldn't have been rehearsed, like the impromptu cover of Chuck Berry's "Around and Around" in Albany that Springsteen called for as the rest of the band thought the show was over. He shouted the chord changes to the band, cried "We're wingin' it!" into the microphone, delighted the crowd with a gloriously sloppy and unplanned performance. (Some moments, though, could have benefited from more rehearsal, like Bob Dylan's bizarro appearance on the last night at Shea, or the time at Fenway Park when Springsteen had to scold Federici for playing the wrong intro to "Frankie.") But no one, not even the members of the E Street Band, can be spontaneous every moment onstage. What they do may be called "playing," but it's "working," too. At least half the set list is the same every night. Most people who see the band are not the crazies, completists, or people who write books. They're normal people who want to be entertained. Mostly, the show is for them. The lighting and audio cues are built around the experience of someone witnessing the band once, not 100 times. The job of a rock'n'roll band is to make the familiar real and, if they're lucky, new. Most nights, that is what Bruce Springsteen and the E Street Band do. "I can't promise you eternal life," Springsteen would shout almost every night on the reunion tour, "but I can promise you life right now!" That line was rehearsed, repeated so often that sometimes Springsteen didn't even need to look down at his teleprompter to get the words right. On their best nights and on their best recordings, Bruce Springsteen and the E Street Band can make something they did 100 times before feel new, to their audience and maybe themselves. That's no dream.

Acknowledgments

The book collects seven essays I wrote about Bruce Springsteen in '04. (*Devils & Dust* was released while this book was in production and is addressed, briefly, only in the introduction.) These essays don't claim to convey anything approaching the whole story of the man and his art, but this book does aim to illuminate some key aspects of his work and career. I'm grateful to all listed below for their support and inspiration, but all failures of reporting and interpretation are mine alone. When you find the inevitable errors, please write me about it and I'll post them, along with the appropriate level of embarrassment, at http://guterman.com/springsteen/, as soon as I get 'em.

When I started talking to Kevin Hanover and Ben Schafer at Da Capo, it was about a far different book, and I thank them for letting me figure out what the right book was. I thank Ben for his many improvements in what you have just read, too. Even before I spoke to the good fellows at Da Capo, this started as a book about the guitarist John Fahey (long story). Glenn Jones, "lektrigdog," and Paul Bryant were enthusiastic supporters of that project. I hope they don't feel abandoned.

My new colleagues Brian Kardon and George Colony and the rest of the team at Forrester didn't know who they were stuck with. Here's my other side, folks.

Publicist extraordinaire Marilyn Laverty and her team have been letting me in to Springsteen concerts and answering obscure questions since . . . well, I will be discreet and not admit how long. No more ridiculous requests, Marilyn, at least until the next tour.

Anyone writing about Springsteen has to figure his way out of the shadow of Dave Marsh. So much of the criticism launched against him has focused on his closeness to his subject, so I want to note that behind any conflicts you'll find tough, smart critical arguments that are almost always worth thinking hard about even when you disagree with them. (His recent essay on "Barbara Allen" in *The Rose and the Briar* is as good as music-writing gets.) I spent a bit of time in his shadow early in my career, and I am grateful for the opportunity. Dave also introduced me to the incomparable Sandy Choron, who will go to Heaven for memorializing T Shirt and Razoo Kelly. More recently, thanks to Chris Phillips and Bill Taylor for vetting some early ideas and approaches, Charles R. Cross for being my northwest doppelganger, and Gary Stewart for revealing the mysteries of the bridge to "Countin' on a Miracle." The indefatigable research of Cross, Phillips, and Erik Flannigan remains essential for anyone who wants to figure out Springsteen's recorded and onstage legacy.

Now that it's finished, I realize I was creating this book in my head long before I tried to put it down on paper. Among the many who had to suffer through me developing my ideas were concert-going buddies from a generation ago, especially Michael Gott and Jill Blackstone. And although I don't talk to him now nearly as much as I'd like to, Andy McLenon, the King of Nashville, did as much to shape my feelings about rock-'n'roll as repeated listenings to Chuck Berry records. Tim Riley is another buddy I don't spend as much time with as I should (and I have less excuse, because he's local). But one night in September '04, after we hadn't seen each other in years, sipping iced tea in the worst restaurant in the Commonwealth of Massachusetts, he dispelled most of my doubts about this book and inspired me to make it worthy of its subject. Mark Caro's tastes lie elsewhere, but he's a peerless friend and a fearless investigator of reunion bands. Dave Yeskel brought me to my first Springsteen concert and remains far too kind and honorable to be as successful as he's been in the record business. My regular unindicted co-conspirator Owen O'Donnell remains an unflagging store of good humor, great ideas, and, 28 years into our friendship, he's still gentle when he deflates a notion I am misguidedly proud of, as he's forced to do every time we speak.

Thanks to my family: Deanna and Ed Schey, John Guterman, and new CD-trading/concert-going buddy

Michael Schey. I'd particularly like to thank Deanna for letting me pursue this music-writing thing even when all external evidence suggested it was a Really Bad Idea. Michael Guterman would have gotten a kick out of how I turned out and I miss him.

This is the first book I've completed since '91, so it's also the first book I've completed since becoming a father. (That's why it took so long?) Eli, Lydia, and Grace motivate, entertain, and astound me every single day, and every now and then they even let us sleep through the night. They're the ideal power trio. Now go clean your rooms.

Back in the late eighties and early nineties, when I wrote too many books about music in too short a time, I left each project so torn and frayed that I couldn't listen to the music I covered in the books for pleasure ever again. (This is a very bad thing if one of your books is about Jerry Lee Lewis.) This is the first time I leave a project hungry to hear more by the performer in question, still discovering new wrinkles with each listen. But I will take a break. Jane Kokernak has lived through nearly 20 years of my listening to Bruce Springsteen's music and talking about it and talking about it and talking about it. It's frustrating when she has more insights in a sentence than I can cough up during a ten-minute monologue, but I've learned to live with that. I promise to shut up now, at least for a while.

About the Author

Jimmy Guterman's five previous books include *12 Days on the Road, The Worst Rock'n'Roll Records of All Time* (with Owen O'Donnell), and *Rockin' My Life Away*. He served as editor-in-chief of *CD Review, Media Unspun*, and *Gaming Industry News*. He is currently editor-in-chief of *Forrester*. He has contributed to more than 100 magazines, among them *Esquire, Fortune, Inside* (where he was a senior editor), *Harvard Business Review, The Industry Standard* (where he was a contributing editor), *Rolling Stone*, and Salon.com. He has produced and annotated many boxed sets, among them collections of Merle Haggard, Loretta Lynn, and Sam and Dave. His current projects include a tribute to the Clash record *Sandinista!*, to be released in December '05, and a novel. He can be reached via http://guterman.com.

Index

237

Index

Index